DAN SCHAFFER

THE SCRIBBLER ™

IMAGE COMICS, INC.

Erik Larsen - *Publisher*
Todd McFarlane - *President*
Marc Silvestri - *CEO*
Jim Valentino - *Vice-President*

Eric Stephenson - *Executive Director*
Jim Demonakos - *PR & Marketing Coordinator*
Mia MacHatton - *Accounts Manager*
Traci Hui - *Administrative Assistant*
Joe Keatinge - *Traffic Manager*
Allen Hui - *Production Manager*
Jonathan Chan - *Production Artist*
Drew Gill - *Production Artist*
Chris Giarrusso - *Production Artist*
www.imagecomics.com

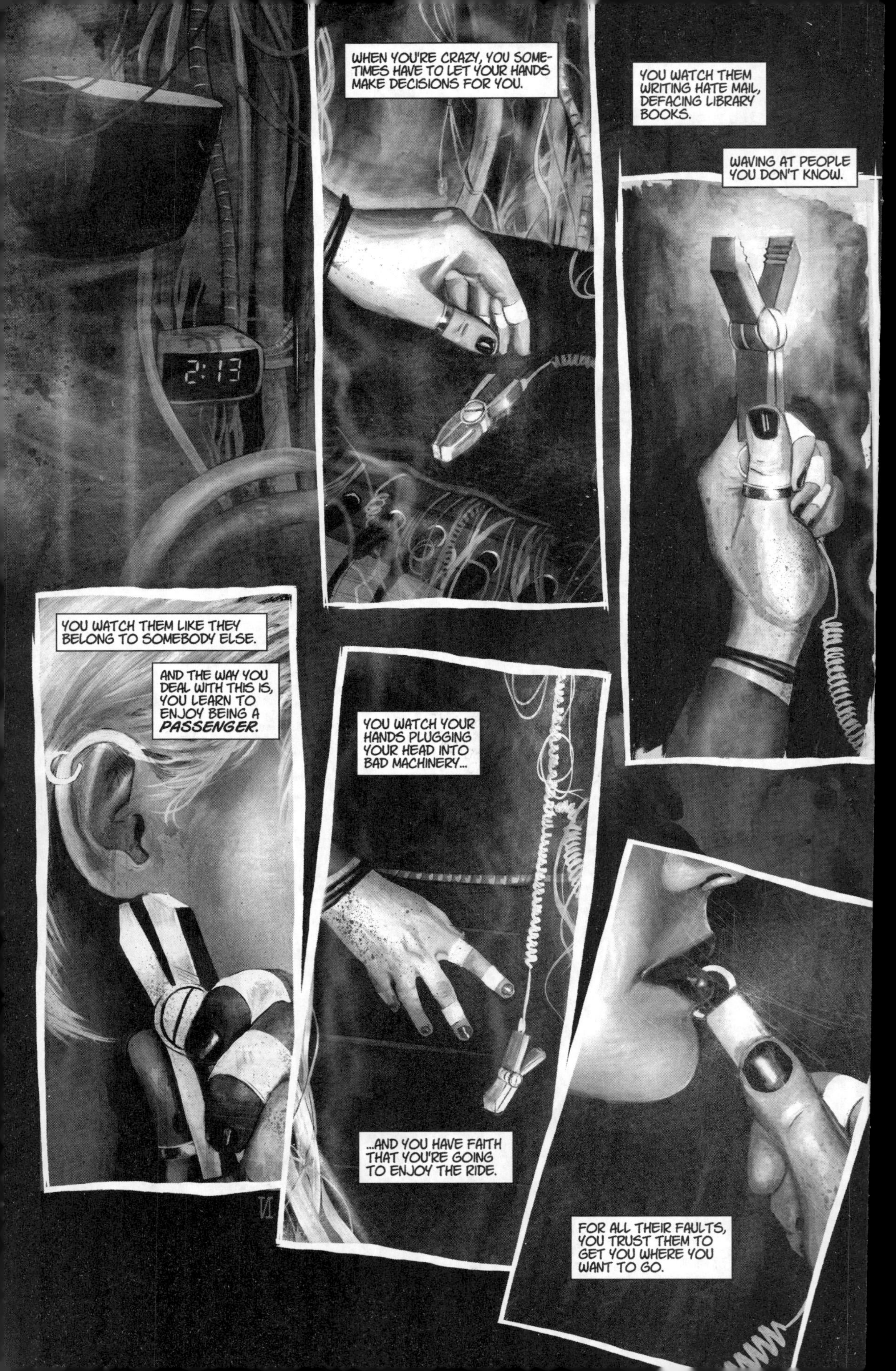
WHEN YOU'RE CRAZY, YOU SOMETIMES HAVE TO LET YOUR HANDS MAKE DECISIONS FOR YOU.
YOU WATCH THEM WRITING HATE MAIL, DEFACING LIBRARY BOOKS.
WAVING AT PEOPLE YOU DON'T KNOW.
YOU WATCH THEM LIKE THEY BELONG TO SOMEBODY ELSE.
AND THE WAY YOU DEAL WITH THIS IS, YOU LEARN TO ENJOY BEING A *PASSENGER*.
YOU WATCH YOUR HANDS PLUGGING YOUR HEAD INTO BAD MACHINERY...
...AND YOU HAVE FAITH THAT YOU'RE GOING TO ENJOY THE RIDE.
FOR ALL THEIR FAULTS, YOU TRUST THEM TO GET YOU WHERE YOU WANT TO GO.

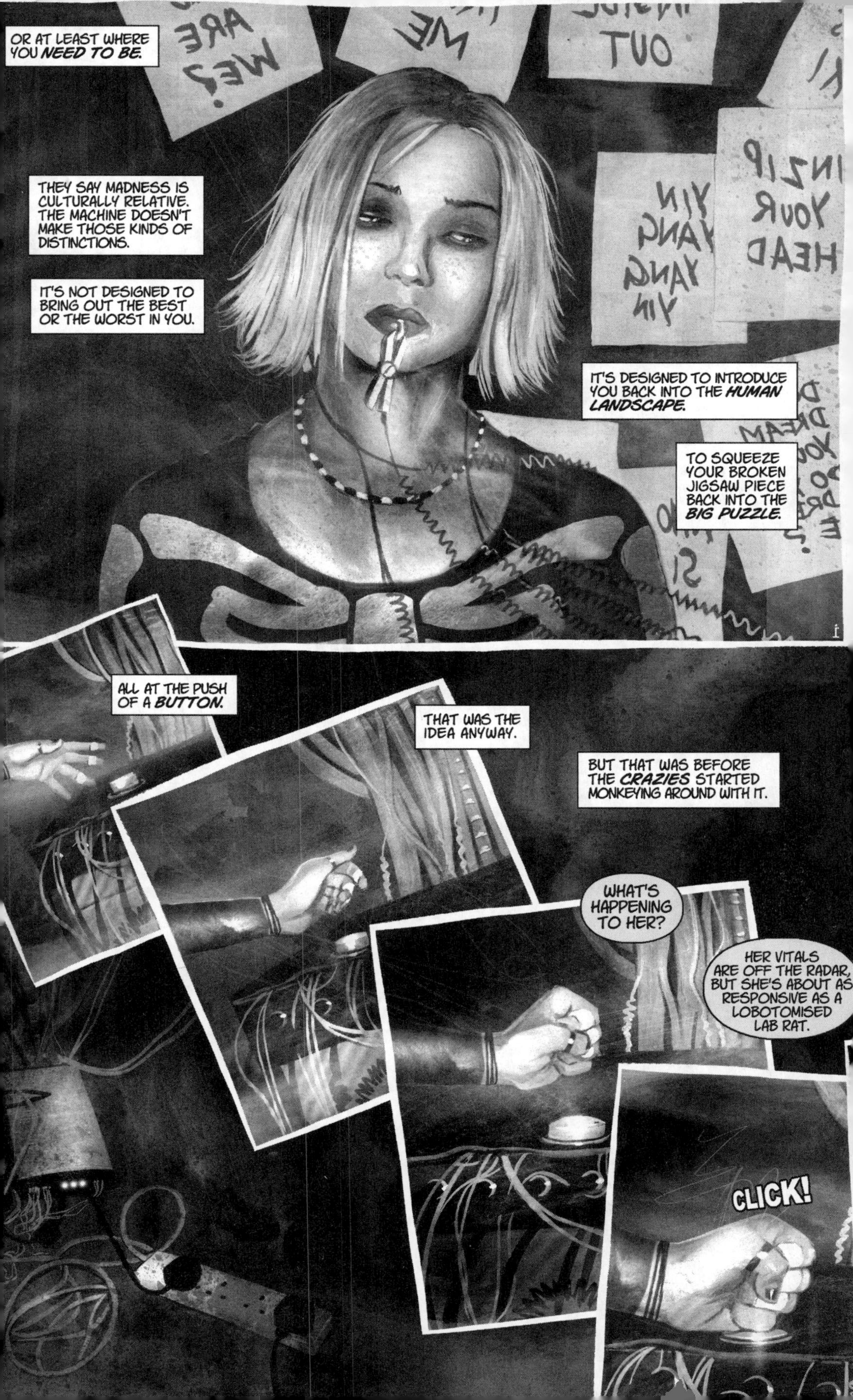
OR AT LEAST WHERE YOU *NEED TO BE.*
THEY SAY MADNESS IS CULTURALLY RELATIVE. THE MACHINE DOESN'T MAKE THOSE KINDS OF DISTINCTIONS.
IT'S NOT DESIGNED TO BRING OUT THE BEST OR THE WORST IN YOU.
IT'S DESIGNED TO INTRODUCE YOU BACK INTO THE *HUMAN LANDSCAPE.*
TO SQUEEZE YOUR BROKEN JIGSAW PIECE BACK INTO THE *BIG PUZZLE.*
ALL AT THE PUSH OF A *BUTTON.*
THAT WAS THE IDEA ANYWAY.
BUT THAT WAS BEFORE THE *CRAZIES* STARTED MONKEYING AROUND WITH IT.
WHAT'S HAPPENING TO HER?
HER VITALS ARE OFF THE RADAR, BUT SHE'S ABOUT AS RESPONSIVE AS A LOBOTOMISED LAB RAT.
CLICK!

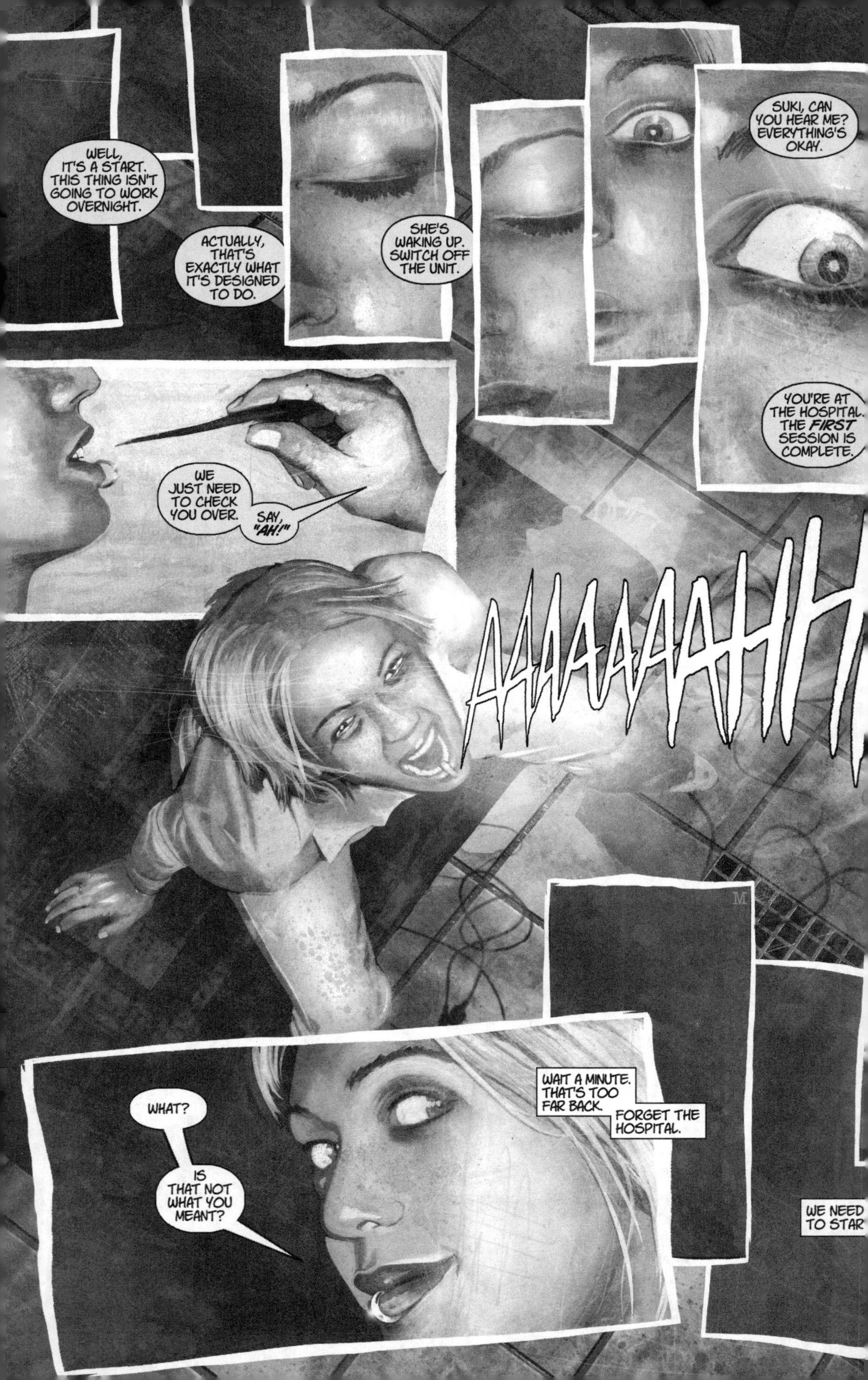
WELL, IT'S A START. THIS THING ISN'T GOING TO WORK OVERNIGHT.
ACTUALLY, THAT'S EXACTLY WHAT IT'S DESIGNED TO DO.
SHE'S WAKING UP. SWITCH OFF THE UNIT.
SUKI, CAN YOU HEAR ME? EVERYTHING'S OKAY.
YOU'RE AT THE HOSPITAL. THE *FIRST* SESSION IS COMPLETE.
WE JUST NEED TO CHECK YOU OVER.
SAY, *"AH!"*
AAAAAAAHH
WHAT?
IS THAT NOT WHAT YOU MEANT?
WAIT A MINUTE. THAT'S TOO FAR BACK.
FORGET THE HOSPITAL.
WE NEED TO STAR

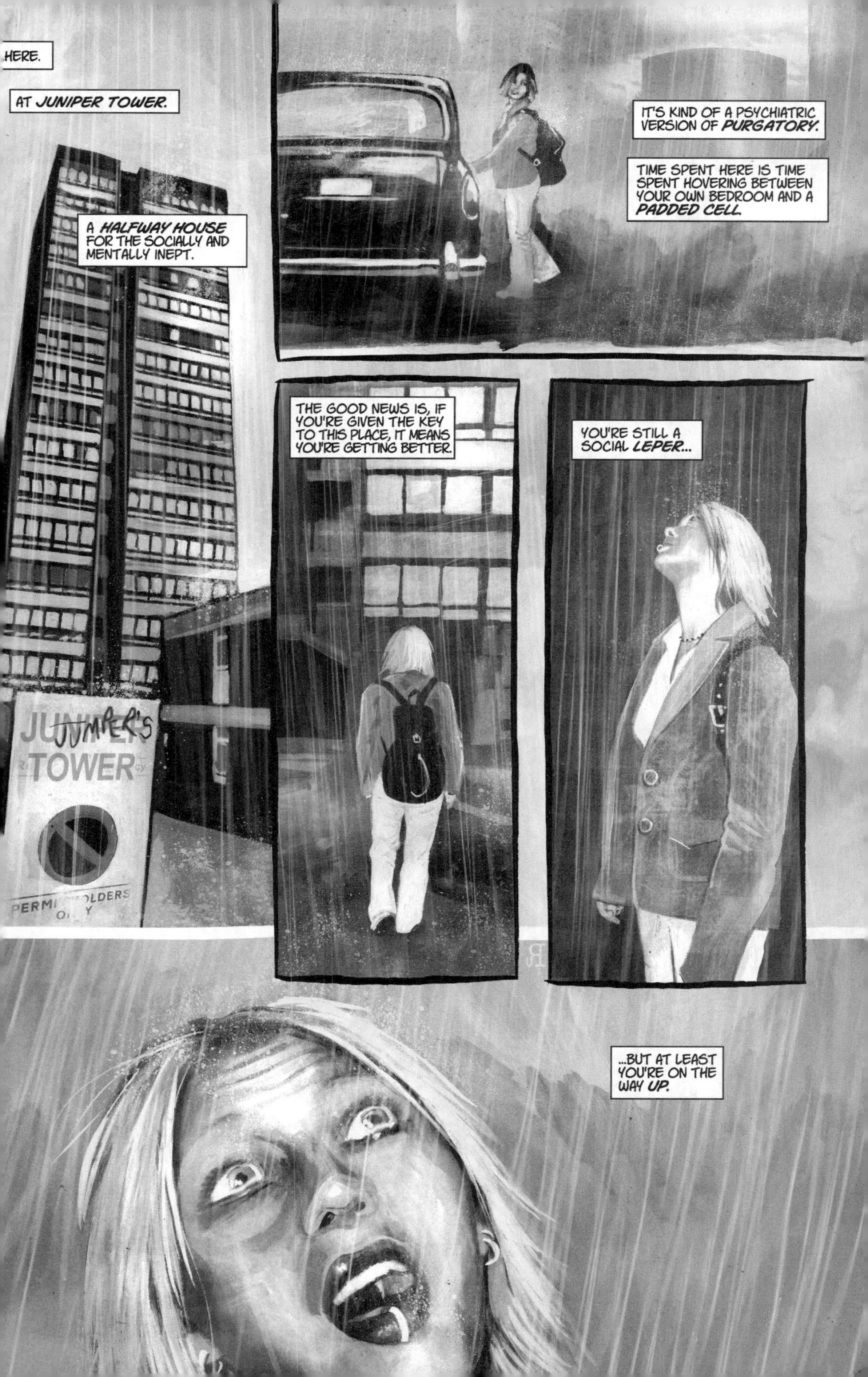
HERE.
AT JUNIPER TOWER.
A HALFWAY HOUSE FOR THE SOCIALLY AND MENTALLY INEPT.
JUMPER'S
TOWER
PERMIT HOLDERS ONLY
IT'S KIND OF A PSYCHIATRIC VERSION OF PURGATORY.
TIME SPENT HERE IS TIME SPENT HOVERING BETWEEN YOUR OWN BEDROOM AND A PADDED CELL.
THE GOOD NEWS IS, IF YOU'RE GIVEN THE KEY TO THIS PLACE, IT MEANS YOU'RE GETTING BETTER.
YOU'RE STILL A SOCIAL LEPER...
...BUT AT LEAST YOU'RE ON THE WAY UP.

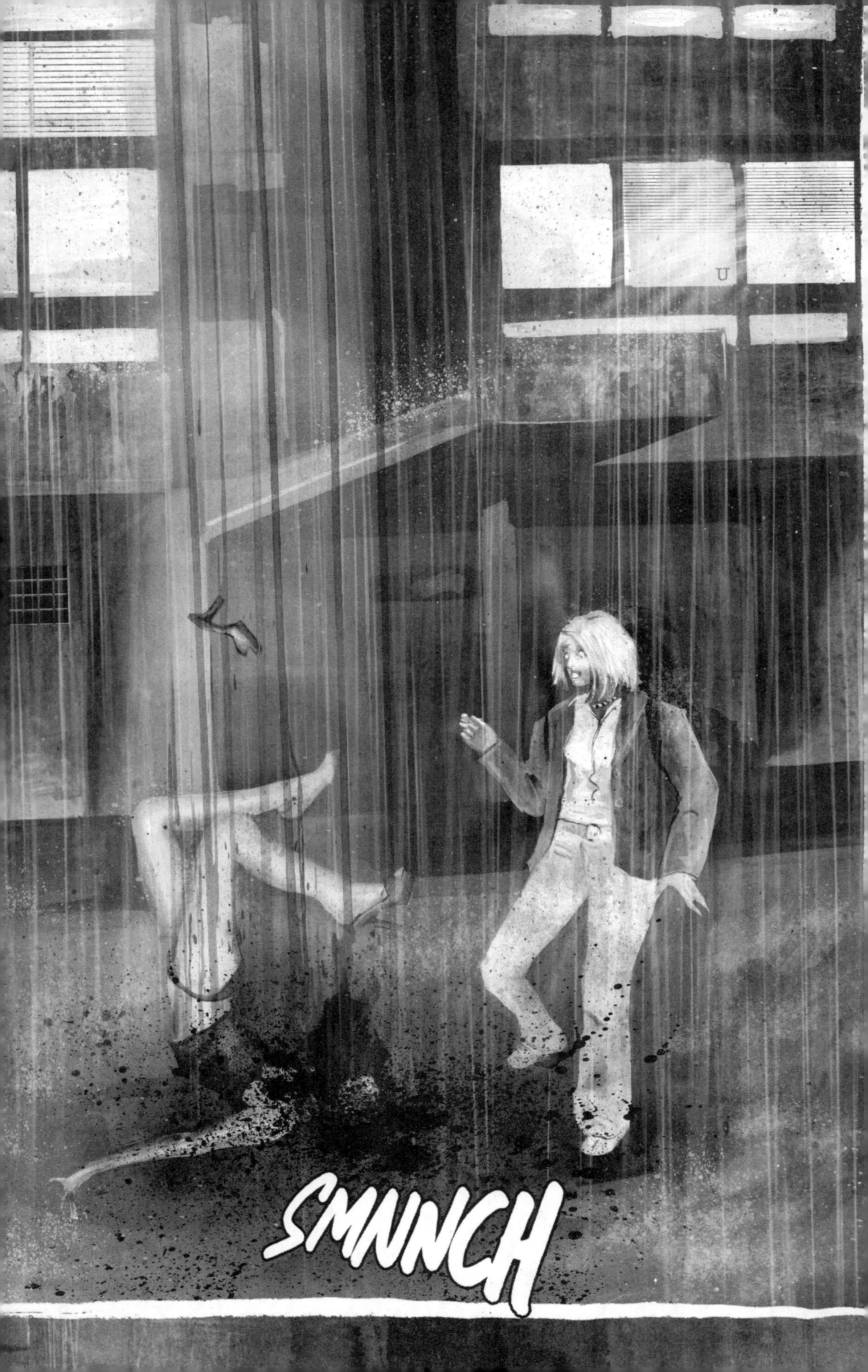
SMUNCH

SIAMESE BURN

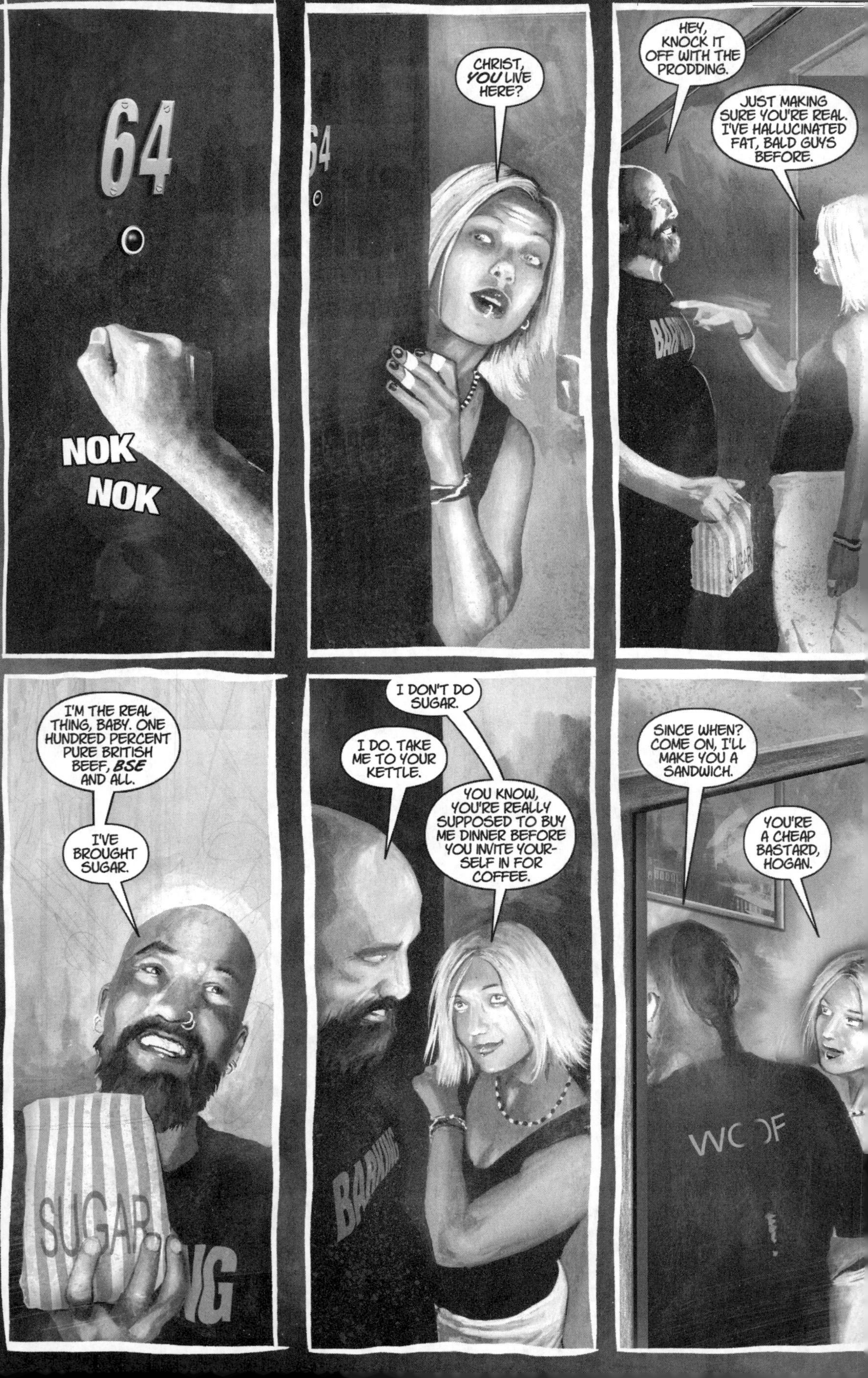
64
NOK NOK
CHRIST, YOU LIVE HERE?
HEY, KNOCK IT OFF WITH THE PRODDING.
JUST MAKING SURE YOU'RE REAL. I'VE HALLUCINATED FAT, BALD GUYS BEFORE.
SUGAR
I'M THE REAL THING, BABY. ONE HUNDRED PERCENT PURE BRITISH BEEF, ***BSE*** AND ALL.
I'VE BROUGHT SUGAR.
I DON'T DO SUGAR.
I DO. TAKE ME TO YOUR KETTLE.
YOU KNOW, YOU'RE REALLY SUPPOSED TO BUY ME DINNER BEFORE YOU INVITE YOURSELF IN FOR COFFEE.
SINCE WHEN? COME ON, I'LL MAKE YOU A SANDWICH.
YOU'RE A CHEAP BASTARD, HOGAN.
WOOF

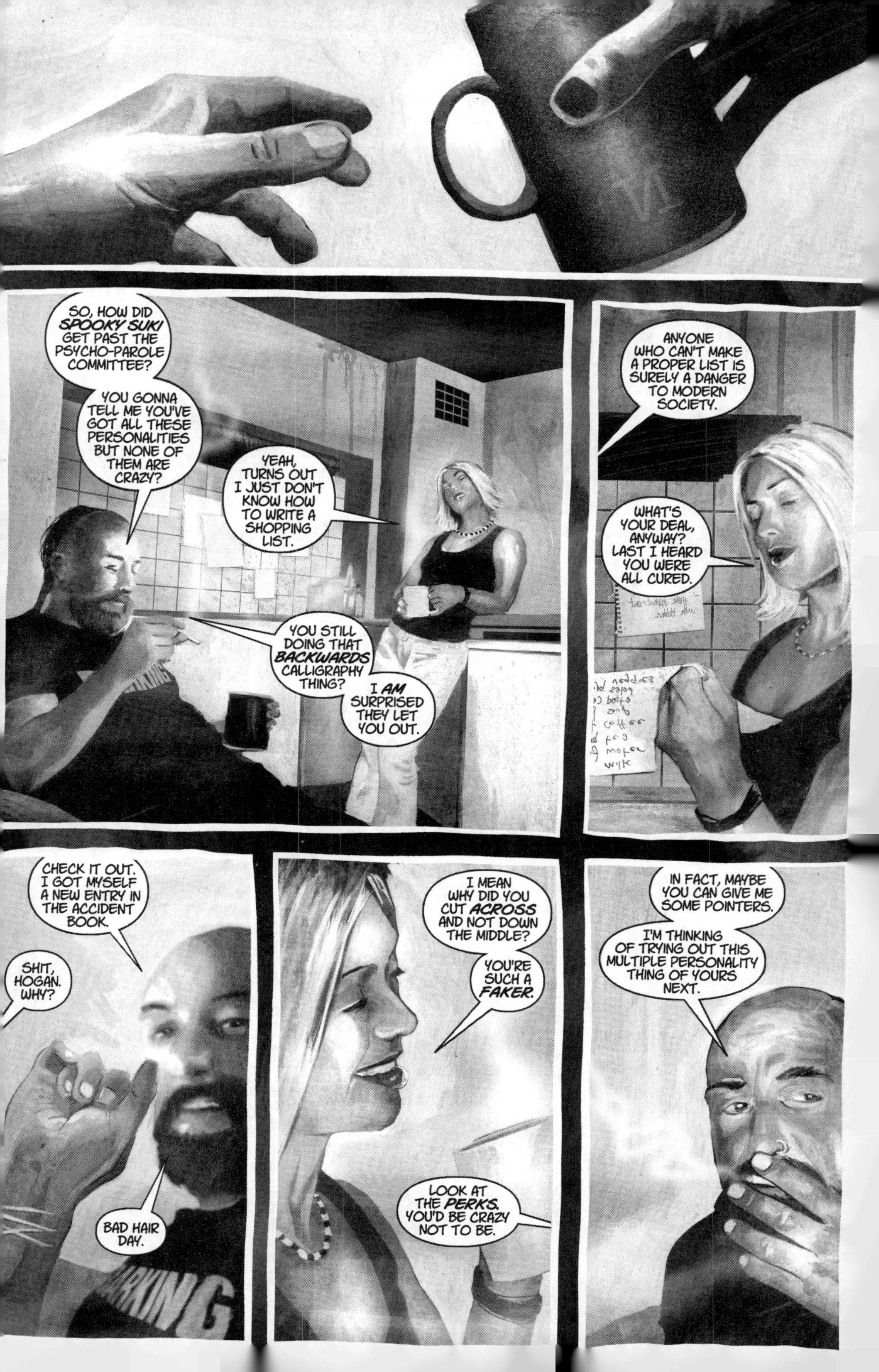
SO, HOW DID SPOOKY SUKI GET PAST THE PSYCHO-PAROLE COMMITTEE?
YOU GONNA TELL ME YOU'VE GOT ALL THESE PERSONALITIES BUT NONE OF THEM ARE CRAZY?
YEAH, TURNS OUT I JUST DON'T KNOW HOW TO WRITE A SHOPPING LIST.
YOU STILL DOING THAT BACKWARDS CALLIGRAPHY THING?
I AM SURPRISED THEY LET YOU OUT.
ANYONE WHO CAN'T MAKE A PROPER LIST IS SURELY A DANGER TO MODERN SOCIETY.
WHAT'S YOUR DEAL, ANYWAY? LAST I HEARD YOU WERE ALL CURED.
CHECK IT OUT. I GOT MYSELF A NEW ENTRY IN THE ACCIDENT BOOK.
SHIT, HOGAN. WHY?
BAD HAIR DAY.
I MEAN WHY DID YOU CUT ACROSS AND NOT DOWN THE MIDDLE?
YOU'RE SUCH A FAKER.
LOOK AT THE PERKS. YOU'D BE CRAZY NOT TO BE.
IN FACT, MAYBE YOU CAN GIVE ME SOME POINTERS.
I'M THINKING OF TRYING OUT THIS MULTIPLE PERSONALITY THING OF YOURS NEXT.

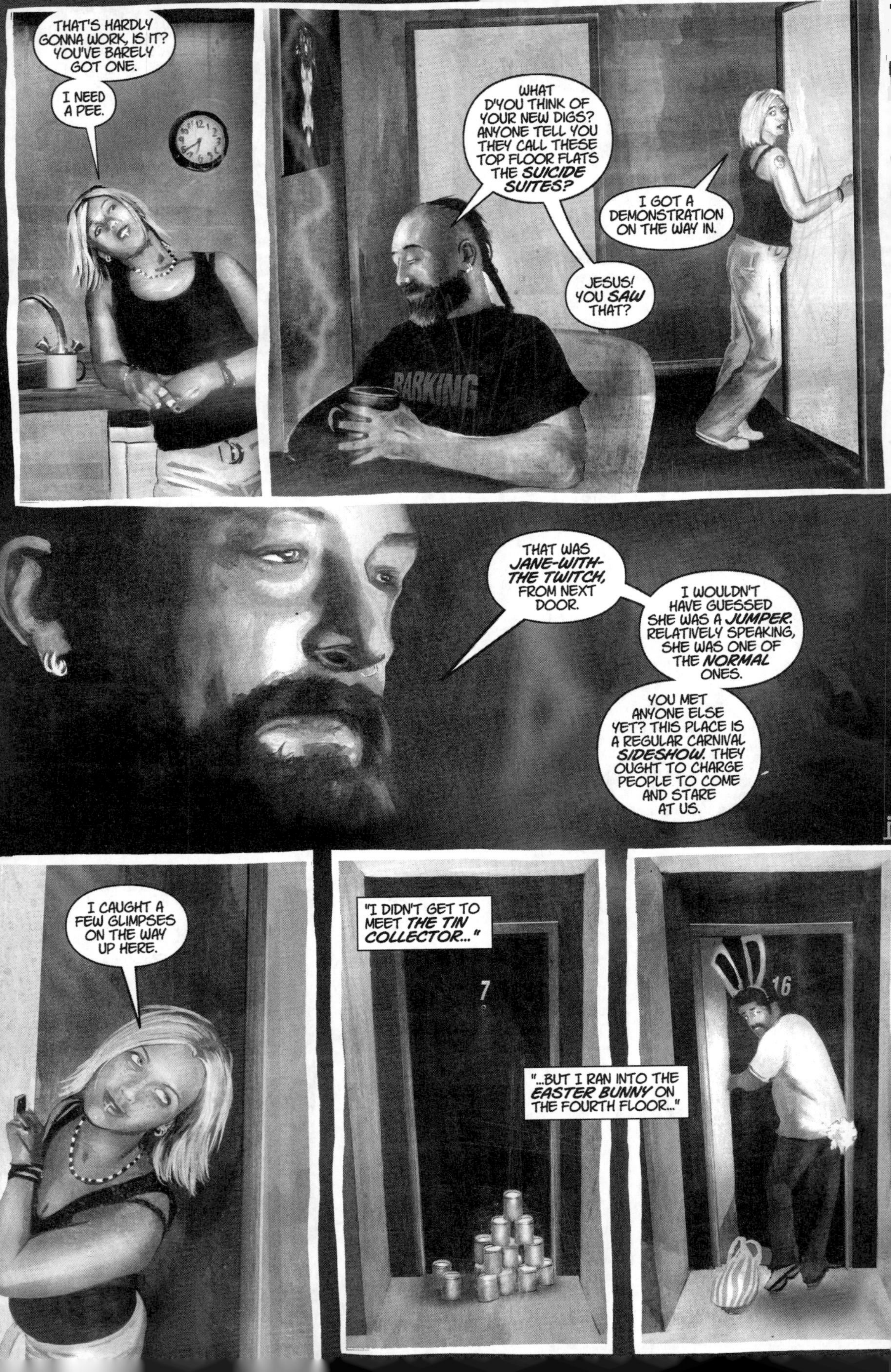

THAT'S HARDLY GONNA WORK, IS IT? YOU'VE BARELY GOT ONE.
I NEED A PEE.
WHAT D'YOU THINK OF YOUR NEW DIGS? ANYONE TELL YOU THEY CALL THESE TOP FLOOR FLATS THE SUICIDE SUITES?
I GOT A DEMONSTRATION ON THE WAY IN.
JESUS! YOU SAW THAT?
PARKING
THAT WAS JANE-WITH-THE TWITCH, FROM NEXT DOOR.
I WOULDN'T HAVE GUESSED SHE WAS A JUMPER. RELATIVELY SPEAKING, SHE WAS ONE OF THE NORMAL ONES.
YOU MET ANYONE ELSE YET? THIS PLACE IS A REGULAR CARNIVAL SIDESHOW. THEY OUGHT TO CHARGE PEOPLE TO COME AND STARE AT US.
I CAUGHT A FEW GLIMPSES ON THE WAY UP HERE.
"I DIDN'T GET TO MEET THE TIN COLLECTOR..."
7
"...BUT I RAN INTO THE EASTER BUNNY ON THE FOURTH FLOOR..."
16

"...AND PICKED UP CLEOPATRA'S SECRET *MILK BATH* RECIPE ON THE FIFTH."

"APPARENLTY, IT'S SEMI-PASTEURISED."

"THE SATANIST ON NINE WASN'T AVAILABLE FOR COMMENT..."

"...BUT *STIGMATA STEVE* SAID HE'S GOT HIM COVERED."

YOU *WALKED* UP HERE?

I DON'T LIKE ELEVATORS.

NEITHER DID *JANE.* SHE WAS SCARED OF EVERYTHING. SMALL SPACES, HEIGHTS, SHE WAS EVEN SCARED OF *ME.* YOU WANNA KNOW THE LAST THING I SAID TO HER?

I SAID I'D LIKE TO SPREAD HER ON MY TOAST. NOW SHE'S STREET JAM. HOW'S *THAT* FOR IRONY?

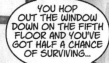

THEY PUT HER ON THE TOP FLOOR FOR A REASON, YOU KNOW? WE'RE ALL SUBJECT TO THE SAME *RISK ASSESSMENT.*

YOU HOP OUT THE WINDOW DOWN ON THE FIFTH FLOOR AND YOU'VE GOT HALF A CHANCE OF SURVIVING...

...BUT YOUR *BUSTED LEGS* ARE GONNA CUT INTO THE CHRISTMAS PARTY BUDGET.

YOU TAKE A SWAN DIVE FROM UP HERE, THOUGH, AND YOU'VE SEEN THE RESULT.

ALL THEY'VE GOT TO WORRY ABOUT IS THE COST OF A *ROAD SWEEPER.*

YOU REMEMBER THAT SERIAL JUMPER ON MY WING BACK AT THE LOONY BIN?

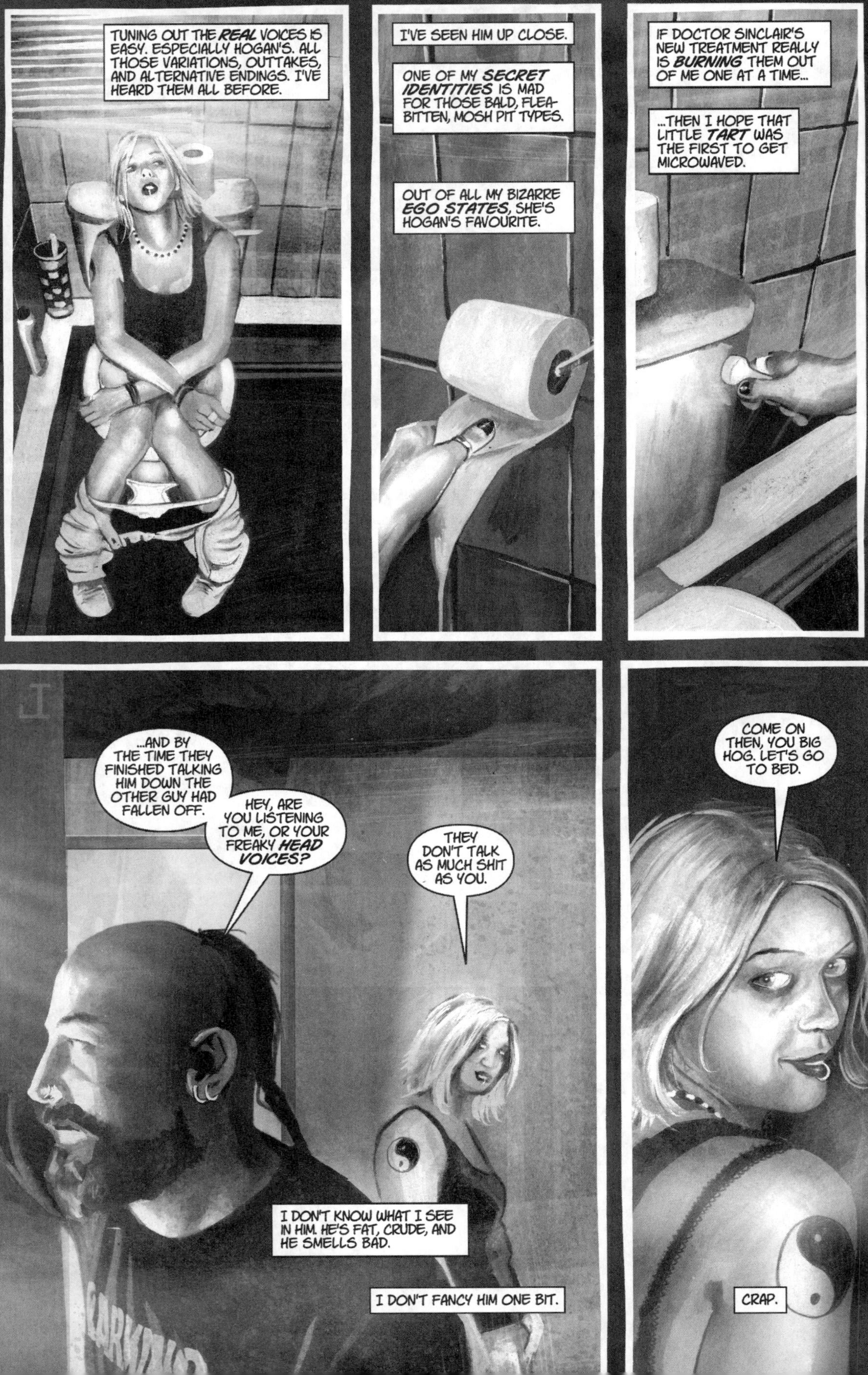
TUNING OUT THE *REAL* VOICES IS EASY. ESPECIALLY HOGAN'S. ALL THOSE VARIATIONS, OUTTAKES, AND ALTERNATIVE ENDINGS. I'VE HEARD THEM ALL BEFORE.
I'VE SEEN HIM UP CLOSE.
ONE OF MY *SECRET IDENTITIES* IS MAD FOR THOSE BALD, FLEA-BITTEN, MOSH PIT TYPES.
OUT OF ALL MY BIZARRE *EGO STATES*, SHE'S HOGAN'S FAVOURITE.
IF DOCTOR SINCLAIR'S NEW TREATMENT REALLY IS *BURNING* THEM OUT OF ME ONE AT A TIME...
...THEN I HOPE THAT LITTLE *TART* WAS THE FIRST TO GET MICROWAVED.
...AND BY THE TIME THEY FINISHED TALKING HIM DOWN THE OTHER GUY HAD FALLEN OFF.
HEY, ARE YOU LISTENING TO ME, OR YOUR FREAKY *HEAD VOICES?*
THEY DON'T TALK AS MUCH SHIT AS YOU.
I DON'T KNOW WHAT I SEE IN HIM. HE'S FAT, CRUDE, AND HE SMELLS BAD.
I DON'T FANCY HIM ONE BIT.
COME ON THEN, YOU BIG HOG. LET'S GO TO BED.
CRAP.

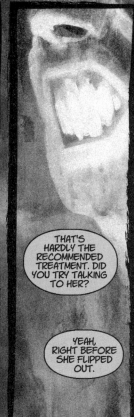

SHE'S HALLUCINATING. YOU WON'T GET ANY SENSE OUT OF HER.

IT'S PROBABLY NOT EVEN HER IN THE DRIVING SEAT.

WHAT SEDATIVES HAVE YOU GOT HER ON?

SEDATIVES DON'T SEEM TO SURPRESS HER *PRIMARY ALTER.* WE HAD TO DOSE HER UP ON ANTI-PSYCHOTICS.

THAT'S HARDLY THE RECOMMENDED TREATMENT. DID YOU TRY TALKING TO HER?

YEAH, RIGHT BEFORE SHE FLIPPED OUT.

MAYBE SHE JUST DOESN'T LIKE YOU.

SUKI, ARE YOU IN THERE? IT'S DOCTOR SINCLAIR.

I WANT YOU TO SIGN THIS CONSENT FORM. CAN YOU DO THAT FOR ME?

CAN YOU SEE THE PEN?

PUT IT IN HER HAND.

IS THAT WISE?

ONLY IF YOU STAND BACK.

THAT'S IT, SUKI. ON THE DOTTED LINE.

GOOD GIRL.

CONSENT

SUKI

THAT'LL HAVE TO DO.

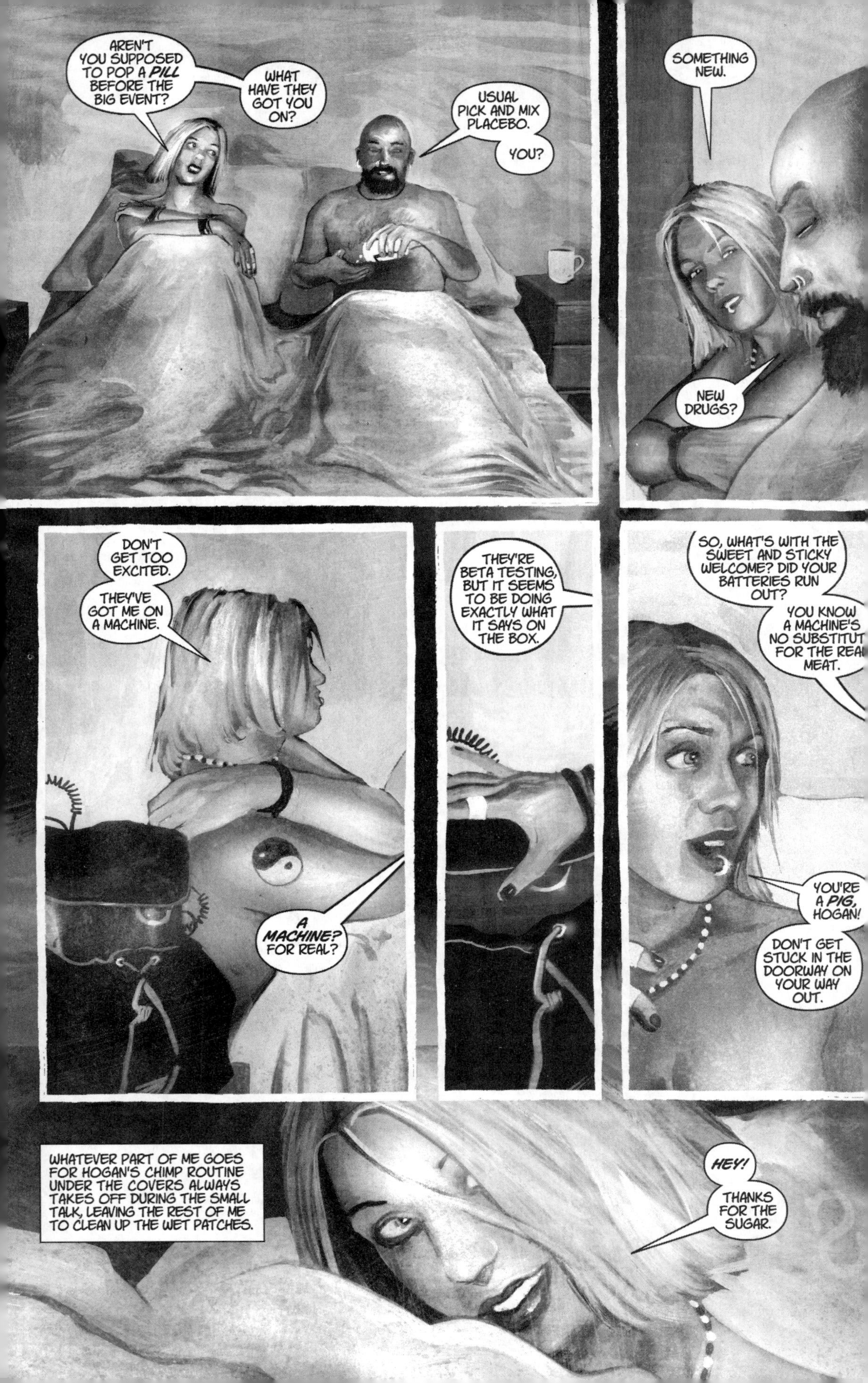
AREN'T YOU SUPPOSED TO POP A PILL BEFORE THE BIG EVENT?
WHAT HAVE THEY GOT YOU ON?
USUAL PICK AND MIX PLACEBO.
YOU?
SOMETHING NEW.
NEW DRUGS?
DON'T GET TOO EXCITED.
THEY'VE GOT ME ON A MACHINE.
A MACHINE? FOR REAL?
THEY'RE BETA TESTING, BUT IT SEEMS TO BE DOING EXACTLY WHAT IT SAYS ON THE BOX.
SO, WHAT'S WITH THE SWEET AND STICKY WELCOME? DID YOUR BATTERIES RUN OUT?
YOU KNOW A MACHINE'S NO SUBSTITUT FOR THE REA MEAT.
YOU'RE A PIG, HOGAN!
DON'T GET STUCK IN THE DOORWAY ON YOUR WAY OUT.
WHATEVER PART OF ME GOES FOR HOGAN'S CHIMP ROUTINE UNDER THE COVERS ALWAYS TAKES OFF DURING THE SMALL TALK, LEAVING THE REST OF ME TO CLEAN UP THE WET PATCHES.
HEY!
THANKS FOR THE SUGAR.

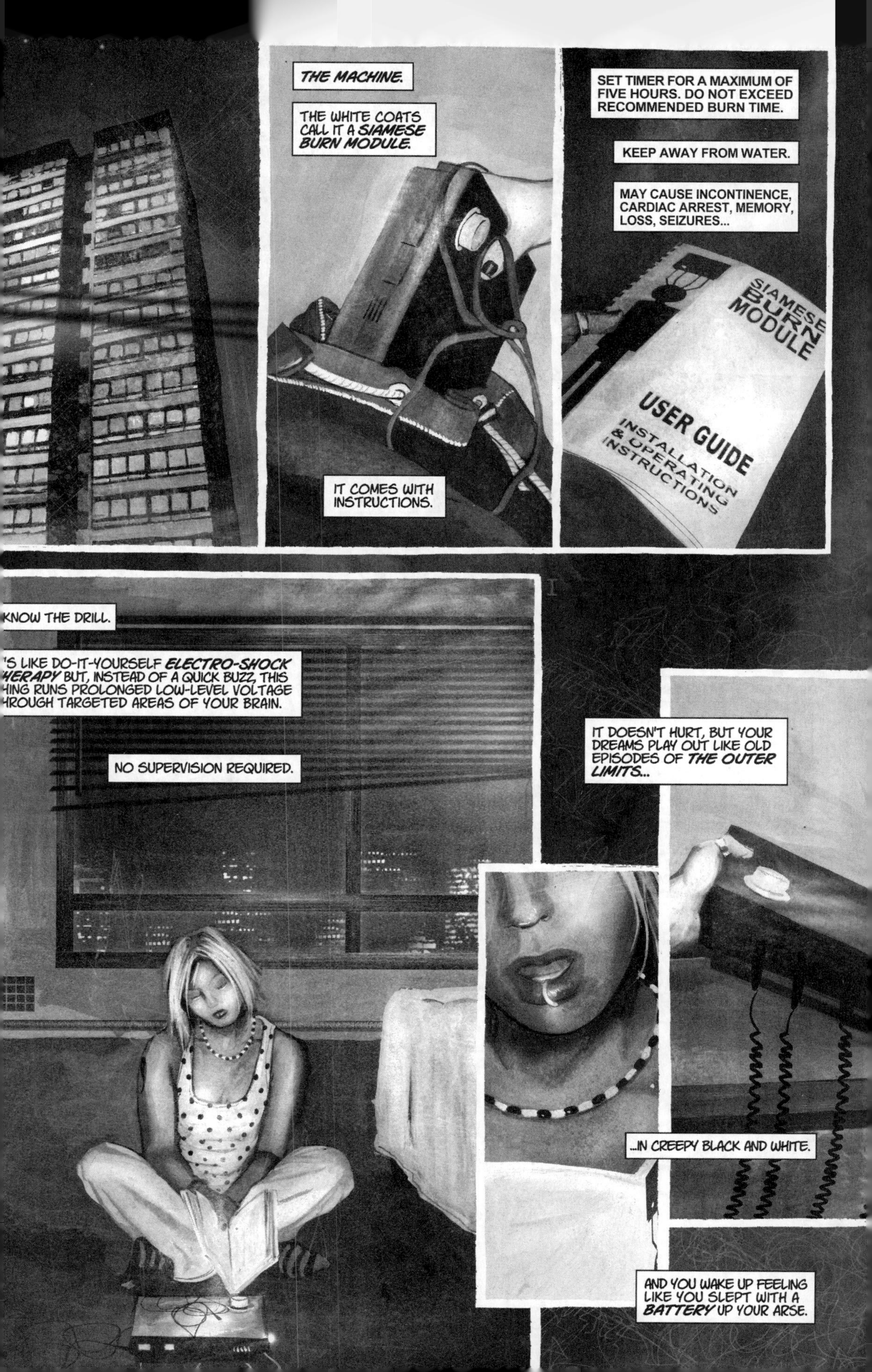
THE MACHINE.
THE WHITE COATS CALL IT A SIAMESE BURN MODULE.
IT COMES WITH INSTRUCTIONS.
SET TIMER FOR A MAXIMUM OF FIVE HOURS. DO NOT EXCEED RECOMMENDED BURN TIME.
KEEP AWAY FROM WATER.
MAY CAUSE INCONTINENCE, CARDIAC ARREST, MEMORY, LOSS, SEIZURES...
SIAMESE BURN MODULE
USER GUIDE
INSTALLATION & OPERATING INSTRUCTIONS
KNOW THE DRILL.
'S LIKE DO-IT-YOURSELF ELECTRO-SHOCK HERAPY BUT, INSTEAD OF A QUICK BUZZ, THIS HING RUNS PROLONGED LOW-LEVEL VOLTAGE HROUGH TARGETED AREAS OF YOUR BRAIN.
NO SUPERVISION REQUIRED.
IT DOESN'T HURT, BUT YOUR DREAMS PLAY OUT LIKE OLD EPISODES OF THE OUTER LIMITS...
...IN CREEPY BLACK AND WHITE.
AND YOU WAKE UP FEELING LIKE YOU SLEPT WITH A BATTERY UP YOUR ARSE.

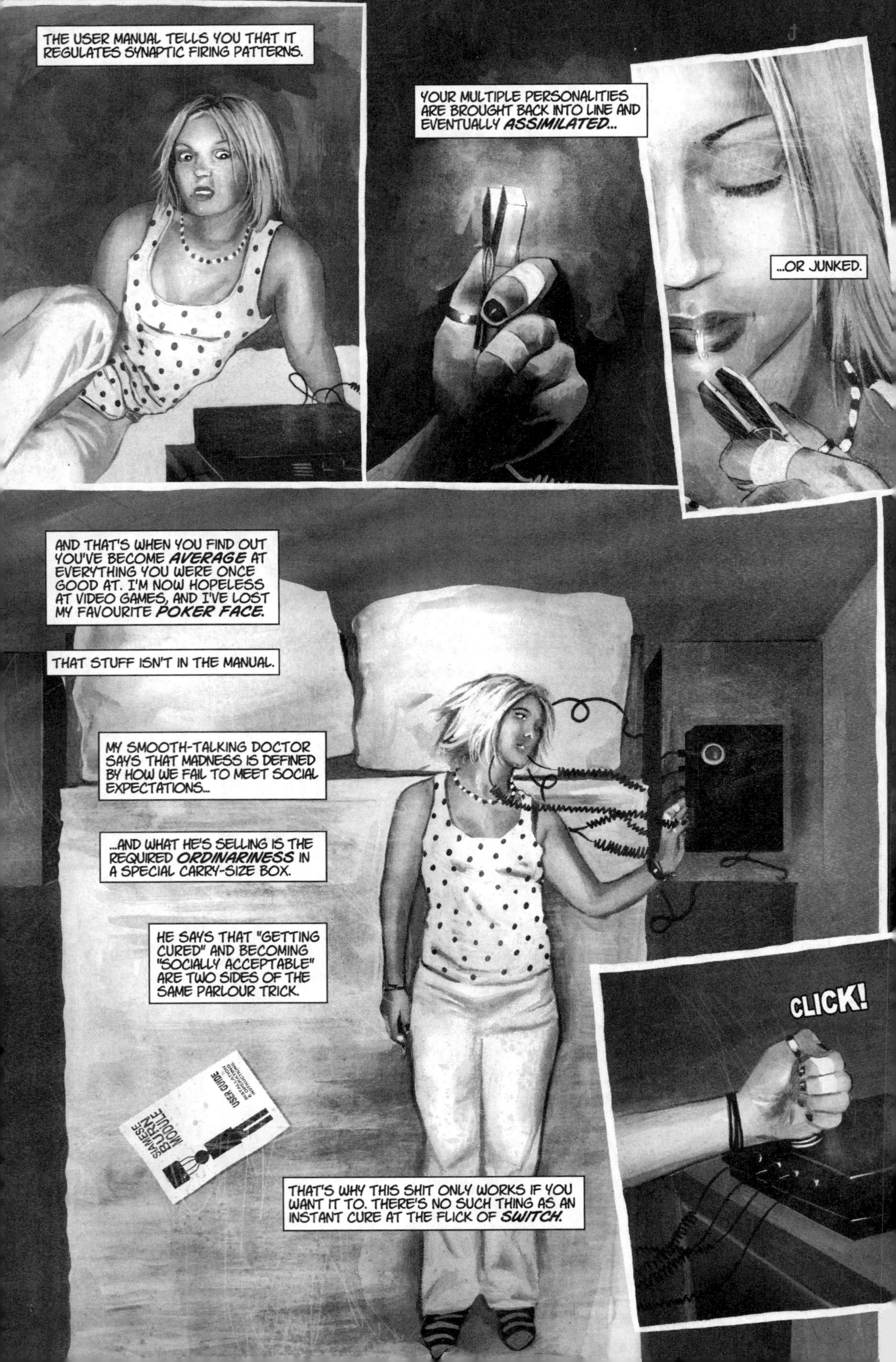

THE USER MANUAL TELLS YOU THAT IT REGULATES SYNAPTIC FIRING PATTERNS.
YOUR MULTIPLE PERSONALITIES ARE BROUGHT BACK INTO LINE AND EVENTUALLY ***ASSIMILATED***...
...OR JUNKED.
AND THAT'S WHEN YOU FIND OUT YOU'VE BECOME ***AVERAGE*** AT EVERYTHING YOU WERE ONCE GOOD AT. I'M NOW HOPELESS AT VIDEO GAMES, AND I'VE LOST MY FAVOURITE ***POKER FACE***.
THAT STUFF ISN'T IN THE MANUAL.
MY SMOOTH-TALKING DOCTOR SAYS THAT MADNESS IS DEFINED BY HOW WE FAIL TO MEET SOCIAL EXPECTATIONS...
...AND WHAT HE'S SELLING IS THE REQUIRED ***ORDINARINESS*** IN A SPECIAL CARRY-SIZE BOX.
HE SAYS THAT "GETTING CURED" AND BECOMING "SOCIALLY ACCEPTABLE" ARE TWO SIDES OF THE SAME PARLOUR TRICK.
SIAMESE BURN MODULE
USER GUIDE
INSTALLATION & OPERATING INSTRUCTIONS
THAT'S WHY THIS SHIT ONLY WORKS IF YOU WANT IT TO. THERE'S NO SUCH THING AS AN INSTANT CURE AT THE FLICK OF ***SWITCH***.
CLICK!

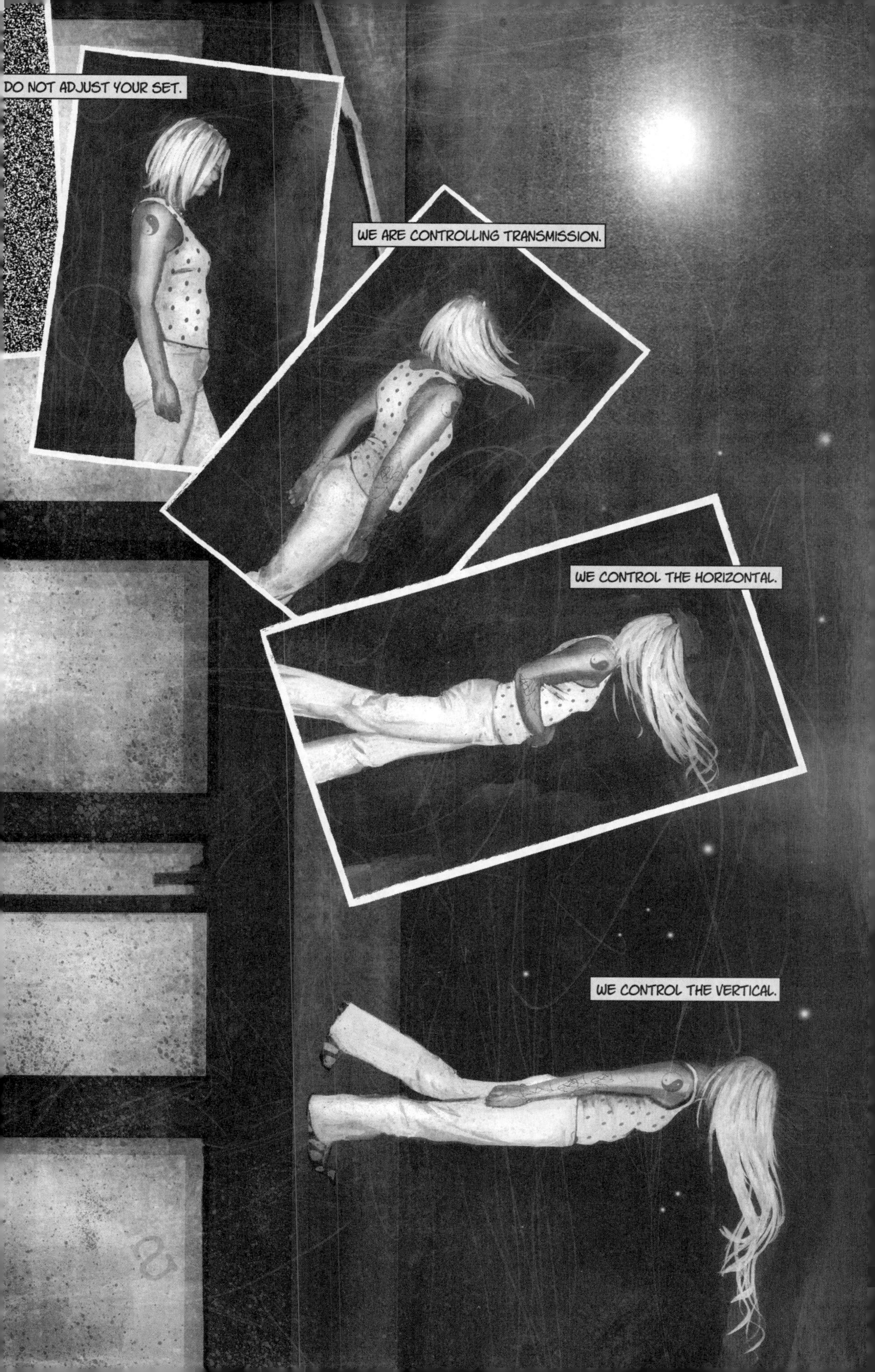
DO NOT ADJUST YOUR SET.
WE ARE CONTROLLING TRANSMISSION.
WE CONTROL THE HORIZONTAL.
WE CONTROL THE VERTICAL.

THE PUSHER

THE PUSHER

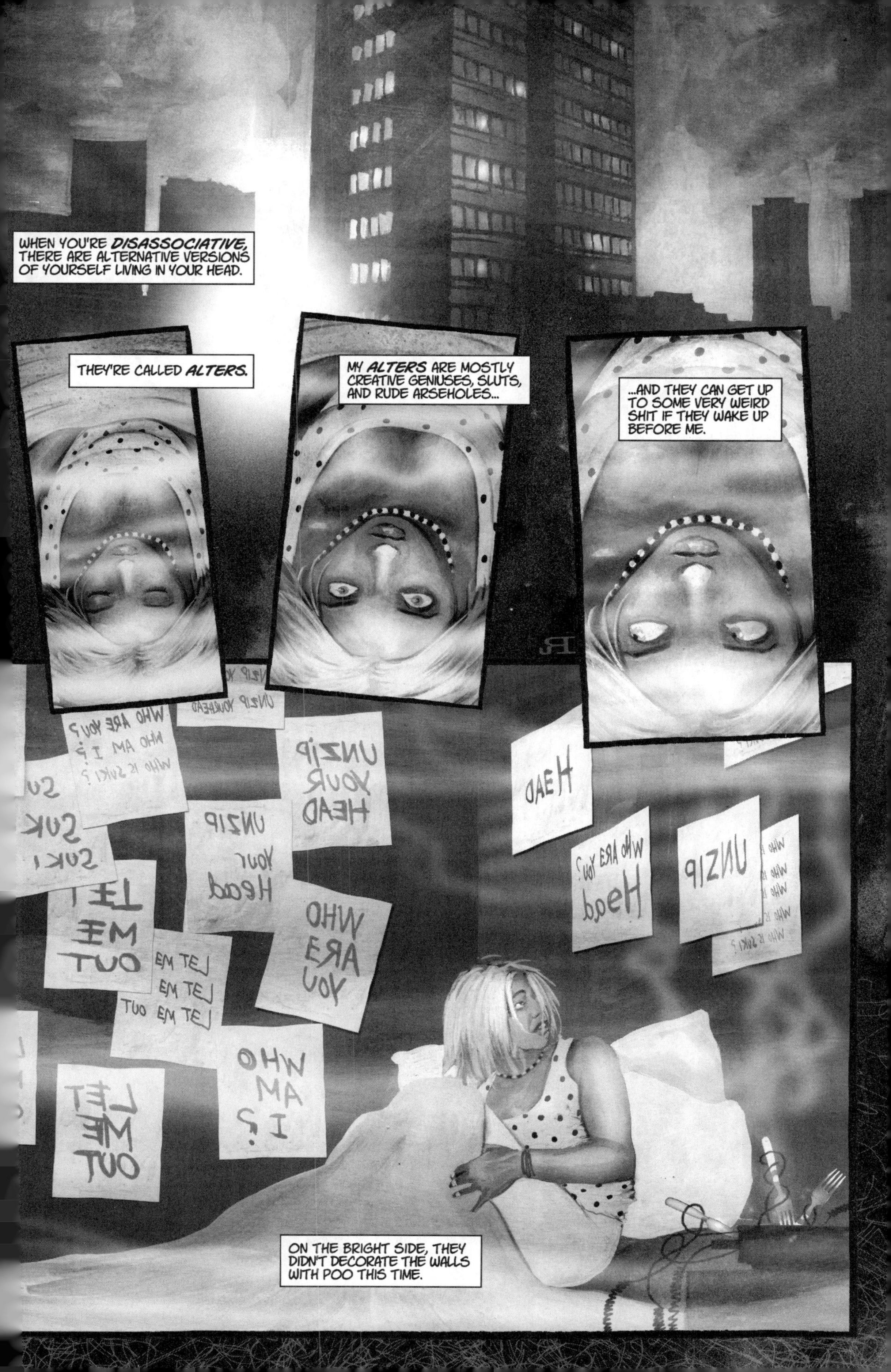
WHEN YOU'RE *DISASSOCIATIVE*, THERE ARE ALTERNATIVE VERSIONS OF YOURSELF LIVING IN YOUR HEAD.
THEY'RE CALLED *ALTERS*.
MY *ALTERS* ARE MOSTLY CREATIVE GENIUSES, SLUTS, AND RUDE ARSEHOLES...
...AND THEY CAN GET UP TO SOME VERY WEIRD SHIT IF THEY WAKE UP BEFORE ME.
ON THE BRIGHT SIDE, THEY DIDN'T DECORATE THE WALLS WITH POO THIS TIME.

WHAT THEY'VE DONE TO *THIS* THING IS ANYBODY'S GUESS.

EITHER ONE OF MY LITTLE *BRAIN BUDDIES* READ A BOOK ON ELECTRONICS WHILE I WASN'T LOOKING...

FZZZ

ZZZT

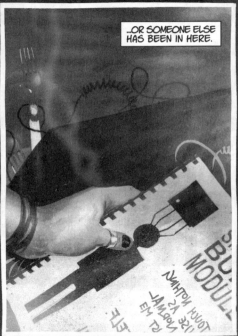

...OR SOMEONE ELSE HAS BEEN IN HERE.

BURN MODULE

OKAY, MY HANDWRITING.

SORT OF.

BURN MODULE

TOUCH NOTHING USE AS NORMAL TRUST ME TRUST YOURSELF.

DEFINITELY NOT MY DOG, THOUGH.

'ALLO.

DON'T LOOK.

DON'T LOOK AND IT WILL GO AWAY.

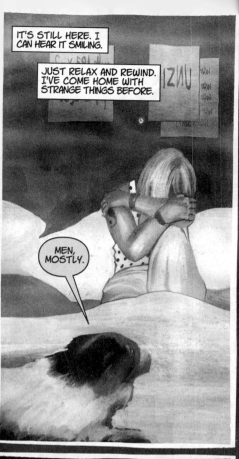

IT'S STILL HERE. I CAN HEAR IT SMILING.

JUST RELAX AND REWIND. I'VE COME HOME WITH STRANGE THINGS BEFORE.

MEN, MOSTLY.

REMEMBER THAT TIME YOU BROUGHT HOME A *WHEEL-CHAIR?*

AND THAT GUY'S PORCH LIGHT?

BRRRRP! BRRRRP!

YEAH, OKAY. THAT DOESN'T MEAN I'M IN THE HABIT OF WAKING UP WITH TALKING *ANIMALS.*

RIGHT.

I'M SURE HOGAN'S GOT *SOME* HUMAN GENES.

BRRRRP! BRRRRP!

HELLO?

BATES MOTEL.

SUKI, IT'S DOCTOR SINCLAIR. IS EVERYTHING OKAY?

WHY? WHAT HAVE YOU HEARD?

I THOUGHT I'D GIVE YOU A *FEW DAYS* TO SETTLE IN BEFORE--

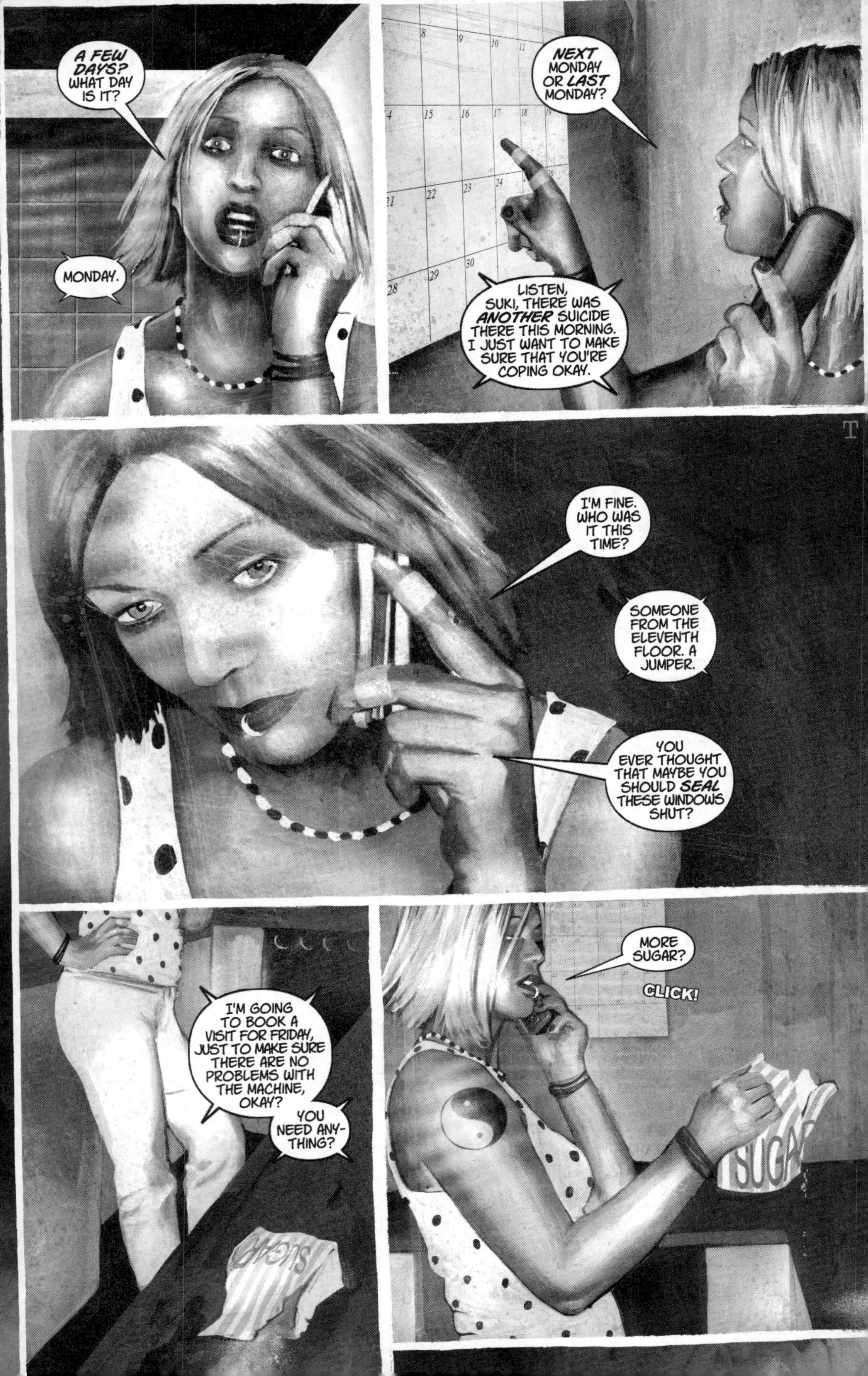
A FEW DAYS? WHAT DAY IS IT?
MONDAY.
NEXT MONDAY OR LAST MONDAY?
LISTEN, SUKI, THERE WAS ANOTHER SUICIDE THERE THIS MORNING. I JUST WANT TO MAKE SURE THAT YOU'RE COPING OKAY.
I'M FINE. WHO WAS IT THIS TIME?
SOMEONE FROM THE ELEVENTH FLOOR. A JUMPER.
YOU EVER THOUGHT THAT MAYBE YOU SHOULD SEAL THESE WINDOWS SHUT?
I'M GOING TO BOOK A VISIT FOR FRIDAY, JUST TO MAKE SURE THERE ARE NO PROBLEMS WITH THE MACHINE, OKAY?
YOU NEED ANYTHING?
SUGAR
MORE SUGAR?
CLICK!
SUGAR

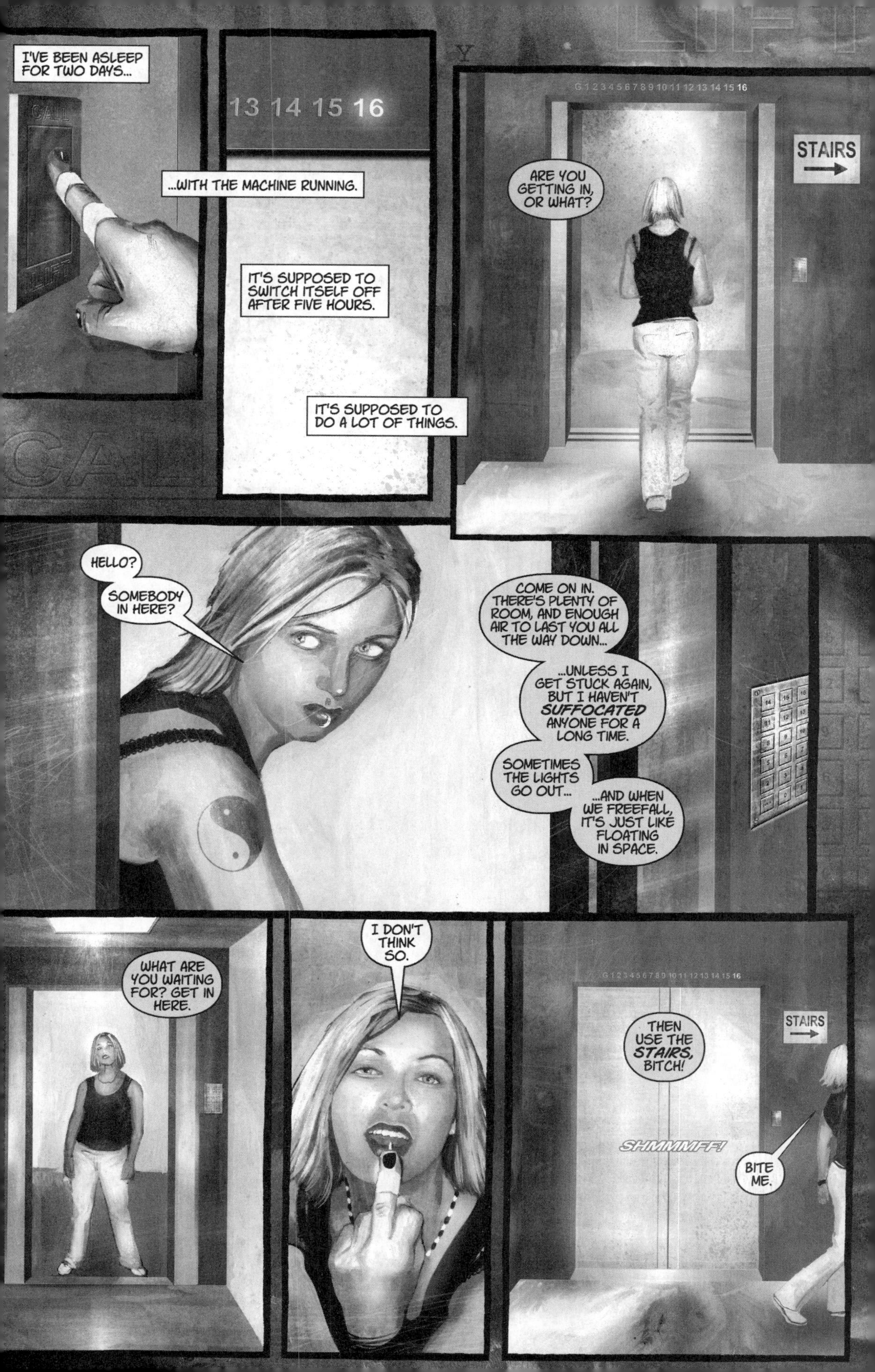
I'VE BEEN ASLEEP FOR TWO DAYS...
...WITH THE MACHINE RUNNING.
13 14 15 16
IT'S SUPPOSED TO SWITCH ITSELF OFF AFTER FIVE HOURS.
IT'S SUPPOSED TO DO A LOT OF THINGS.
G 1 2 3 4 5 6 7 8 9 10 11 12 13 14 15 16
STAIRS
ARE YOU GETTING IN, OR WHAT?
HELLO?
SOMEBODY IN HERE?
COME ON IN. THERE'S PLENTY OF ROOM, AND ENOUGH AIR TO LAST YOU ALL THE WAY DOWN...
...UNLESS I GET STUCK AGAIN, BUT I HAVEN'T SUFFOCATED ANYONE FOR A LONG TIME.
SOMETIMES THE LIGHTS GO OUT...
...AND WHEN WE FREEFALL, IT'S JUST LIKE FLOATING IN SPACE.
WHAT ARE YOU WAITING FOR? GET IN HERE.
I DON'T THINK SO.
G 1 2 3 4 5 6 7 8 9 10 11 12 13 14 15 16
STAIRS
THEN USE THE STAIRS, BITCH!
SHMMMFF!
BITE ME.

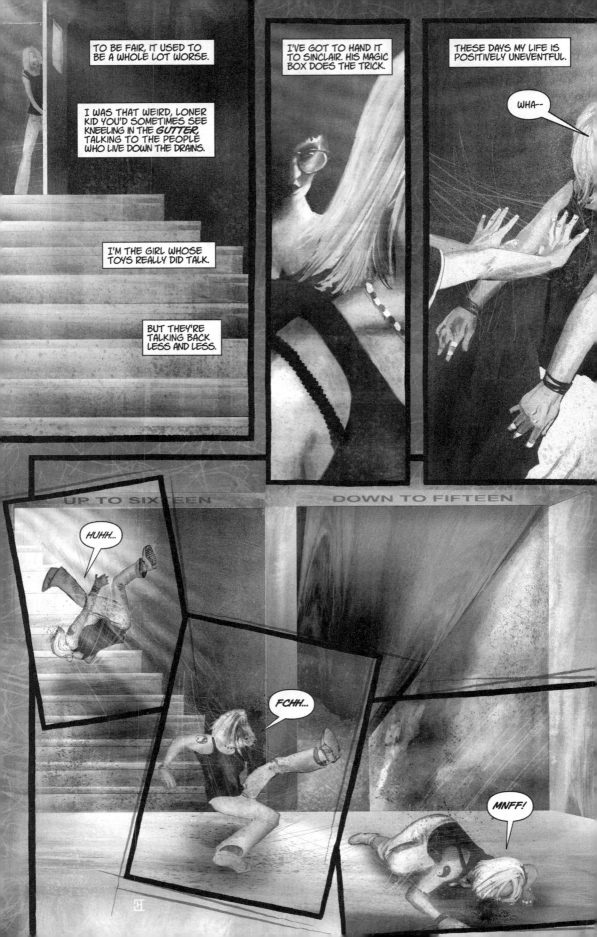

TO BE FAIR, IT USED TO BE A WHOLE LOT WORSE.

I WAS THAT WEIRD, LONER KID YOU'D SOMETIMES SEE KNEELING IN THE *GUTTER* TALKING TO THE PEOPLE WHO LIVE DOWN THE DRAINS.

I'M THE GIRL WHOSE TOYS REALLY DID TALK.

BUT THEY'RE TALKING BACK LESS AND LESS.

I'VE GOT TO HAND IT TO SINCLAIR. HIS MAGIC BOX DOES THE TRICK.

THESE DAYS MY LIFE IS POSITIVELY UNEVENTFUL.

WHA--

UP TO SIXTEEN

DOWN TO FIFTEEN

HUHH...

FCHH...

MNFF!

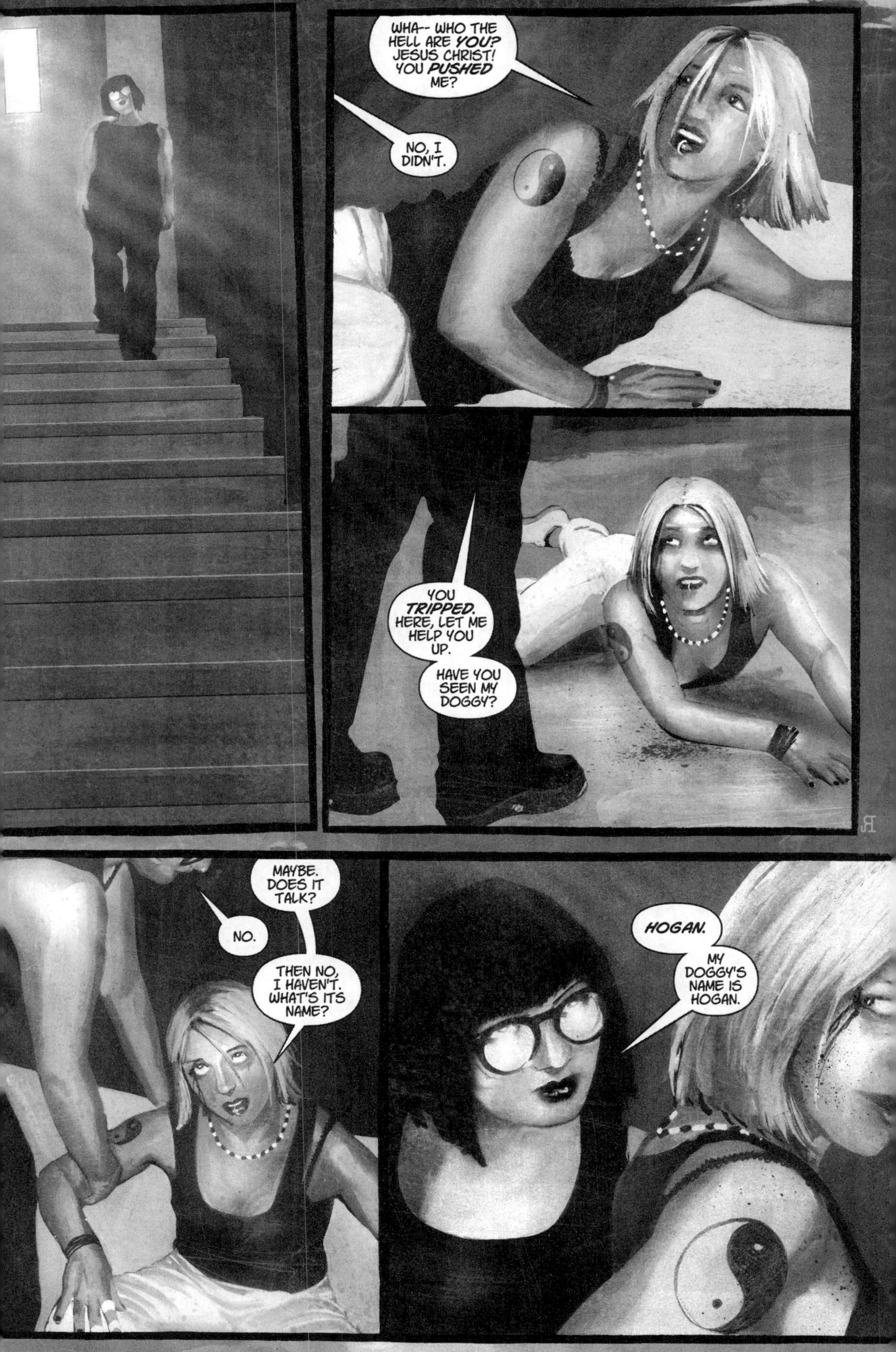
WHA-- WHO THE HELL ARE *YOU?* JESUS CHRIST! YOU *PUSHED* ME?
NO, I DIDN'T.
YOU *TRIPPED*. HERE, LET ME HELP YOU UP.
HAVE YOU SEEN MY DOGGY?
MAYBE. DOES IT TALK?
NO.
THEN NO, I HAVEN'T. WHAT'S ITS NAME?
HOGAN.
MY DOGGY'S NAME IS HOGAN.

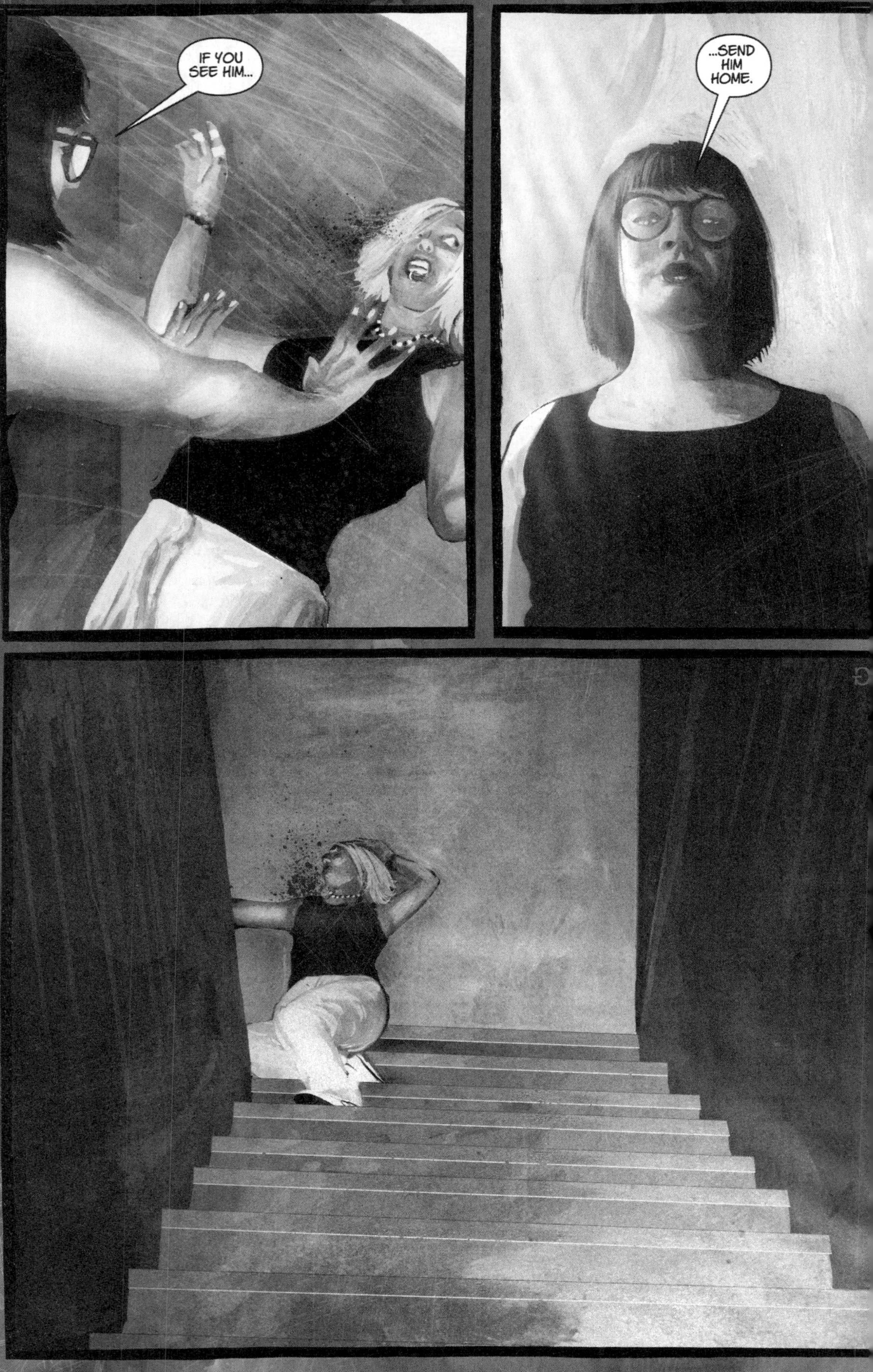
IF YOU SEE HIM...
...SEND HIM HOME.

3.
FRIENDS

FRIENDS

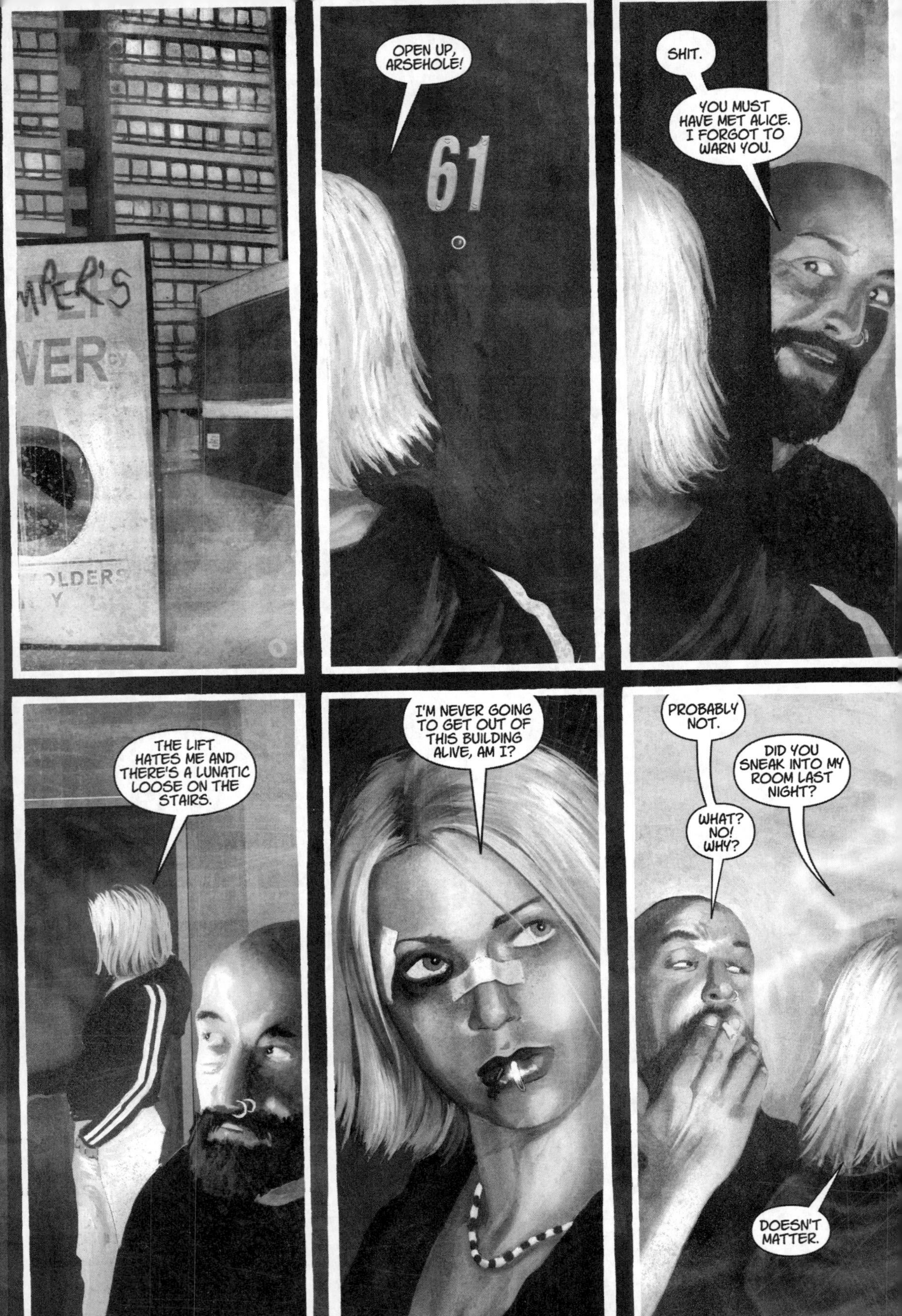
OPEN UP, ARSEHOLE!
SHIT.
YOU MUST HAVE MET ALICE. I FORGOT TO WARN YOU.
THE LIFT HATES ME AND THERE'S A LUNATIC LOOSE ON THE STAIRS.
I'M NEVER GOING TO GET OUT OF THIS BUILDING ALIVE, AM I?
PROBABLY NOT.
DID YOU SNEAK INTO MY ROOM LAST NIGHT?
WHAT? NO! WHY?
DOESN'T MATTER.

I SEE YOU'RE STILL *MUTILATING* DEFENCELESS RADIOS.

I HAVE GADGETS.

I HOPE YOU DIDN'T GIVE THEM TO ME.

I RIGGED AN AERIAL UP ON THE ROOF. YOU WOULD NOT BELIEVE THE THINGS YOU CAN HEAR UP HERE.

DISTANT NUMBERS STATIONS, BACKWARDS MUSIC CHANNELS, ANGELS AND DEMONS TALKING TO EACH OTHER THROUGH THE WHITE NOISE.

HERE. HAVE A LISTEN.

...ALMOST DOWN TO JUST THE TWO OF YOU... THE YIN AND THE YANG... SHE'S BIGGER THAN YOU THINK AND IT'S SO TIGHT IN HERE... SHE COULD SPRING OUT OF THE TOP OF YOUR HEAD LIKE A JACK IN THE BOX.

UNZIP YOUR HEAD.

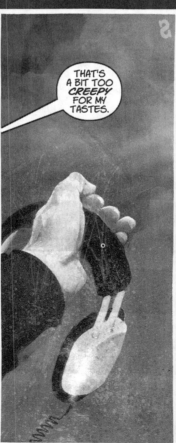

THAT'S A BIT TOO *CREEPY* FOR MY TASTES.

I HAVEN'T PLUGGED IT IN YET.

HEH! UHM... SO, LOOK, I NEED TO BORROW A VIDEO CAMERA.

IF YOU'RE THINKING OF TRYING TO CATCH ALICE'S ANTICS ON FILM, FORGET IT. NOBODY'S GOING TO CARE.

EVERYONE KNOWS SHE'S A COMPULSIVE PUSHER. IT'S EASIER TO JUST STAY OFF THE STAIRS.

IT'S NOTHING TO DO WITH HER. IT'S FOR A PROJECT.

NOT THE HOME PORN THING AGAIN?

RELAX, I'M NOT GOING TO MESS UP YOUR EQUIPMENT.

PASS ME THAT TRIPOD TOO.

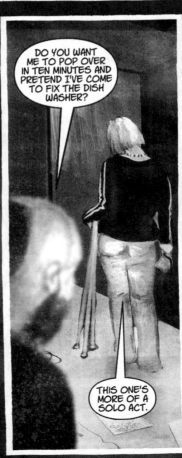

DO YOU WANT ME TO POP OVER IN TEN MINUTES AND PRETEND I'VE COME TO FIX THE DISH WASHER?

THIS ONE'S MORE OF A SOLO ACT.

YOU'RE GOING TO BE NO FUN WHEN YOU'RE CURED.

MAKE ME A COPY?

YOU'VE MADE GOOD PROGRESS WITH THE *SIAMESE BURN*, SUKI. THE SIDE EFFECTS ARE MINIMAL.

YOUR ALTERS SEEM TO HAVE CALMED DOWN TO A MANAGEABLE LEVEL. WE THINK MOST OF THEM HAVE BEEN ERADICATED.

WE'RE READY TO MOVE YOU OUT OF HERE AND INTO YOUR OWN FLAT.

WE CAN LET YOU TAKE A *MODULE* HOME, HAVE A CHANCE AT A NORMAL LIFE.

WHAT DO YOU SAY?

ARE YOU READY TO GO HOME?

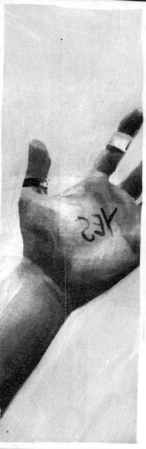

SURE. WE'RE READY.

I MEAN, I'M READY.

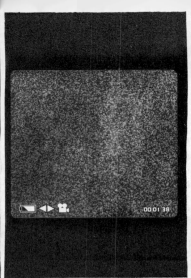

...AND THEN SHE PUSHED ME AGAIN.

CAN YOU BELIEVE THAT?

SHE'S GOT A WARPED SENSE OF HUMOUR. THAT'S WHY I MOVED OUT.

SO, ARE WE READY TO DO THIS THING?

COME ON. PUSH THE BUTTON.

I'LL BARK IF I SEE YOUR BRAINS COMING OUTTA YOUR NOSE.

AND THIS IS HOW YOUR WORLD SPIRALS INWARDS. THEY TELL YOU TO *FIGHT* THE VOICES, BUT THE VOICES DON'T PACK UP AND GO HOME AT FIVE-THIRTY.

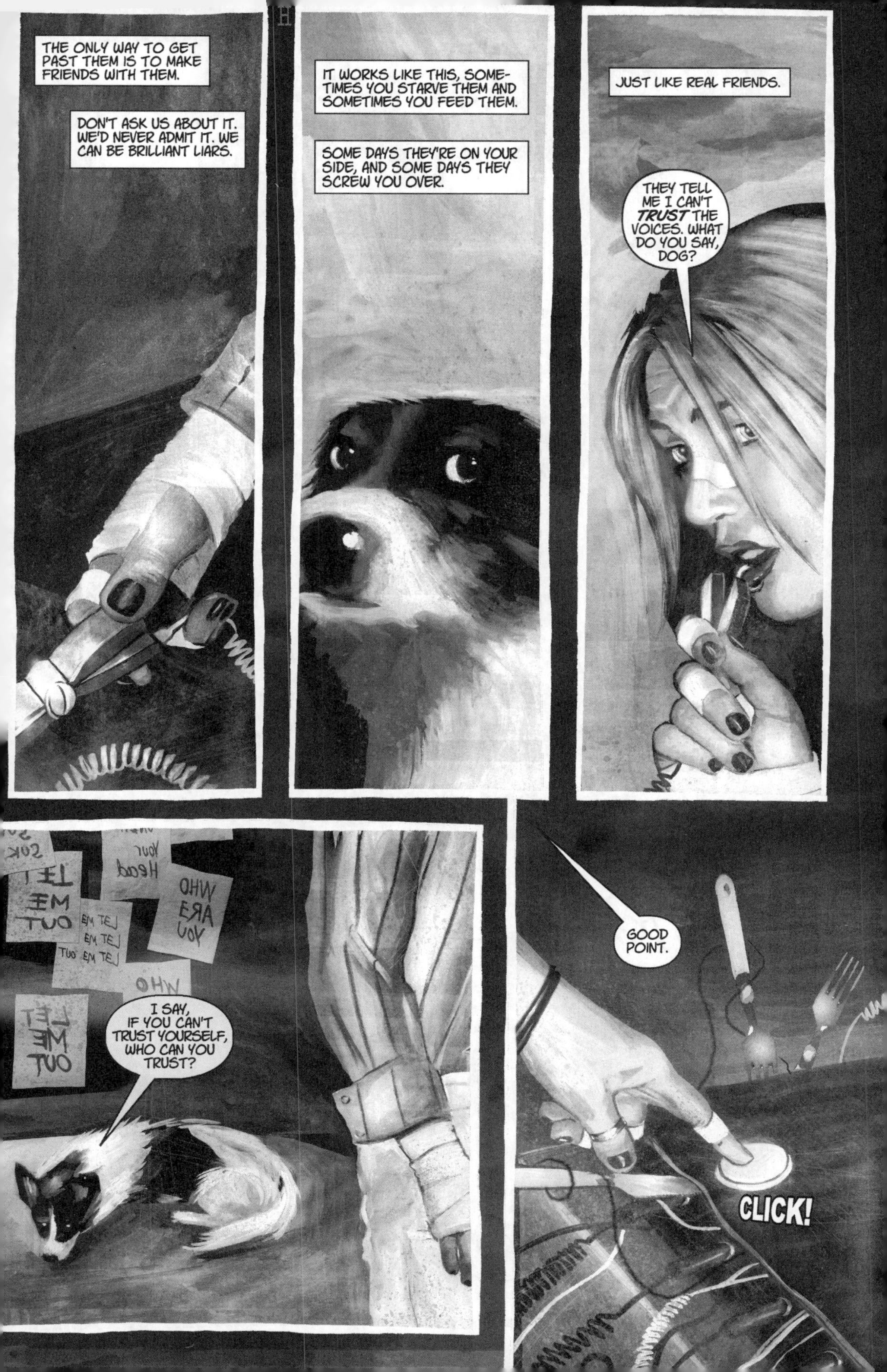
THE ONLY WAY TO GET PAST THEM IS TO MAKE FRIENDS WITH THEM.
DON'T ASK US ABOUT IT. WE'D NEVER ADMIT IT. WE CAN BE BRILLIANT LIARS.
IT WORKS LIKE THIS, SOMETIMES YOU STARVE THEM AND SOMETIMES YOU FEED THEM.
SOME DAYS THEY'RE ON YOUR SIDE, AND SOME DAYS THEY SCREW YOU OVER.
JUST LIKE REAL FRIENDS.
THEY TELL ME I CAN'T TRUST THE VOICES. WHAT DO YOU SAY, DOG?
I SAY, IF YOU CAN'T TRUST YOURSELF, WHO CAN YOU TRUST?
GOOD POINT.
CLICK!

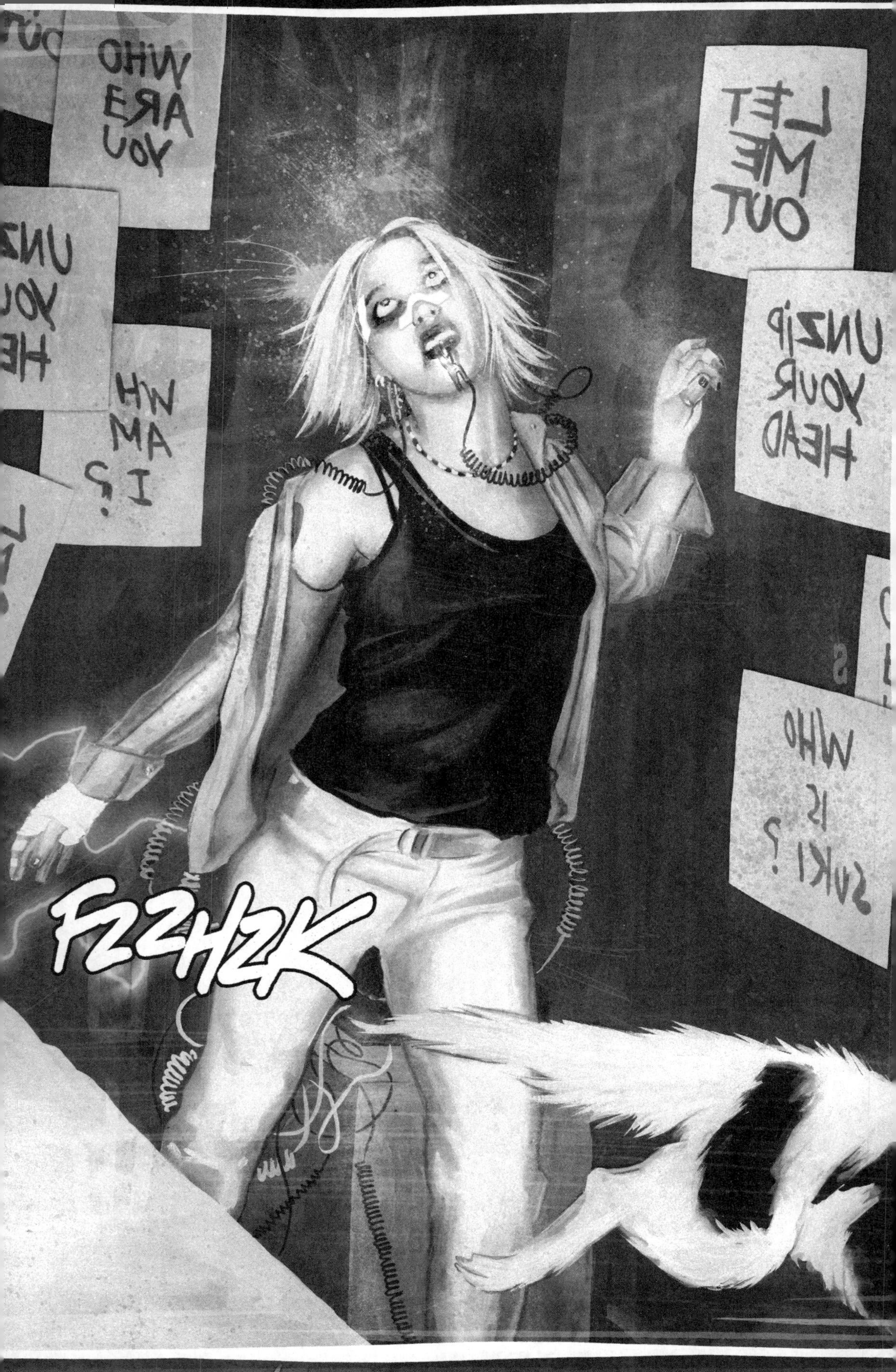
WHO ARE YOU
WHO AM I?
LET ME OUT
UNZIP YOUR HEAD
WHO IS SUKI?
FZZHZK

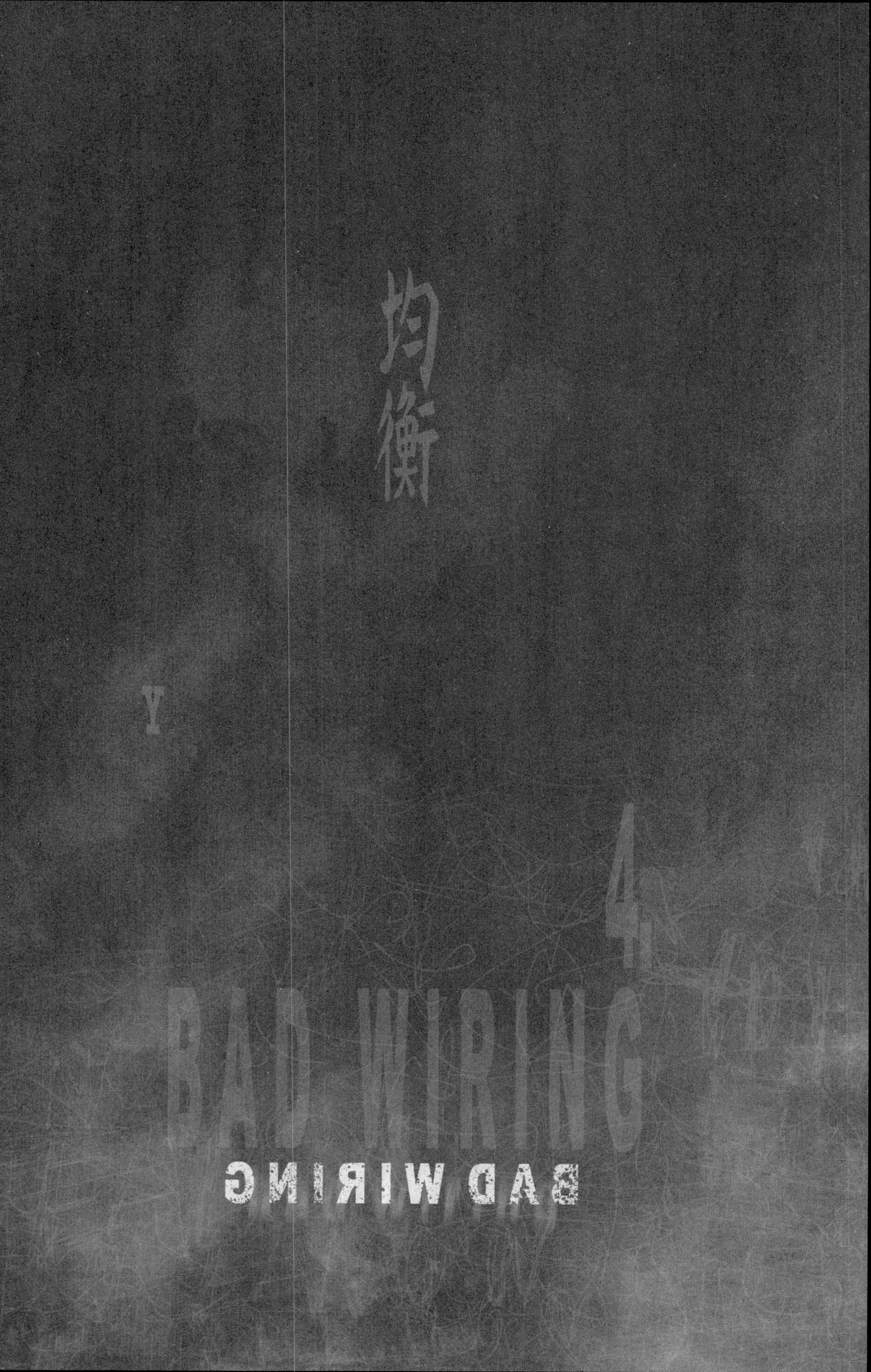
均衡
4
BAD WIRING

WHERE ARE WE WITH THE TALK THERAPY PROGRAM?
NOWHERE. THE SIAMESE BURN IS THE ONLY THING THAT'S WORKING.
IT'S BEEN SUCCESSFULLY USED TO REMOVE ONE OF HER MORE EXTRAVAGANT PERSONALITIES.
REALLY? WHICH ONE?
THE INTERIOR DECORATOR. THERE'S BEEN NO FAECAL ART IN HER ROOM FOR WEEKS NOW.
THE ONLY SIDE EFFECT WE'VE MONITORED IS AN INCREASE IN ACTIVITY FROM THE SCRIBBLER.
IT SEEMS TO BE FILLING UP THE EMPTY SPACE LEFT BEHIND BY THE DISSOLUTION OF THE OTHER ALTER.
THE SCRIBBLER?
IT'S HER MOST EXTREME EGO STATE. THE ONE THAT LEAVES CRYPTIC MESSAGES WRITTEN BACKWARDS ALL OVER THE WALLS.
WE BELIEVE THAT, IF WE CAN BURN THAT ONE OUT, HER PRIMARY IDENTITY WILL FALL INTO THE GAP LEAVING HER WITH AN ACCEPTABLE LEVEL OF MENTAL HEALTH.
DO YOU CONCUR?
BUGGERED IF I KNOW. I MAY HAVE INVENTED THAT MACHINE, BUT I'M JUST WINGING IT HERE.
I STILL CAN'T BELIEVE THE BLOODY THING ACTUALLY WORKS.

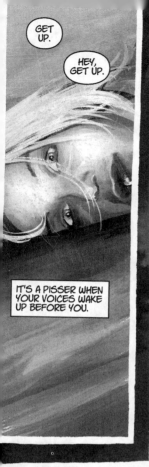

GET UP.

HEY, GET UP.

IT'S A PISSER WHEN YOUR VOICES WAKE UP BEFORE YOU.

THOSE DAYS START OFF WEIRD AND DON'T SLOW DOWN UNTIL THEY HIT CRAZY TOWN.

COME ON. GET OFF THE STREET!

THE STREET?

CARE IN THE COMMUNITY, MY ARSE! MY TAX MONEY SHOULD BE GOING TO STARVING CHILDREN OR SICK PUPPIES, NOT SPONGERS LIKE YOU.

GET A JOB, NUTTER!

USUALLY THERE WOULD BE AT LEAST ONE VOICE TELLING ME TO KICK THIS ARSEHOLE IN THE BALLS.

BUT NOT TODAY.

WEDNESDAY?

TWO DAYS.

I'VE LOST TWO DAYS.

Wednesday 18th

AGAIN.

PNG!

I HEARD YOU WERE AFRAID OF LIFTS.

IS THAT SUPPOSED TO BE FUNNY?

WHAT ARE YOU DOING UP HERE?

LOOKING FOR MY DOG. ARE YOU SURE YOU HAVEN'T SEEN HIM?

PRETTY SURE.

HE'S GOT FLEAS, YOU KNOW. FLEAS AND TICKS.

AND A SHOCKING CASE OF RABIES.

THAT WHY YOU NAMED HIM HOGAN?

DOG FOOD

HOGAN'S MY FRIEND. WE'VE BEEN FRIENDS SINCE BEFORE YOU GOT HERE.

EVERYTHING WAS OKAY BEFORE YOU SHOWED UP. DID YOU KNOW SOMEBODY ELSE JUMPED LAST NIGHT?

FIVE MINUTES AFTER YOU MOV EVERYONE STAR DIVING OUT T WINDOWS. WH DOES THAT TELL YOU?

MY DEODORANT DOESN'T WORK?

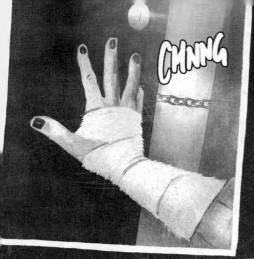

CHNNG

THE SECURITY CHAIN'S ON.

BUT YOU'RE OUT HERE.

BHMMF!

YOU LOCKED YOURSELF OUT...

...FROM THE INSIDE?

JUST HOW CRAZY ARE YOU?

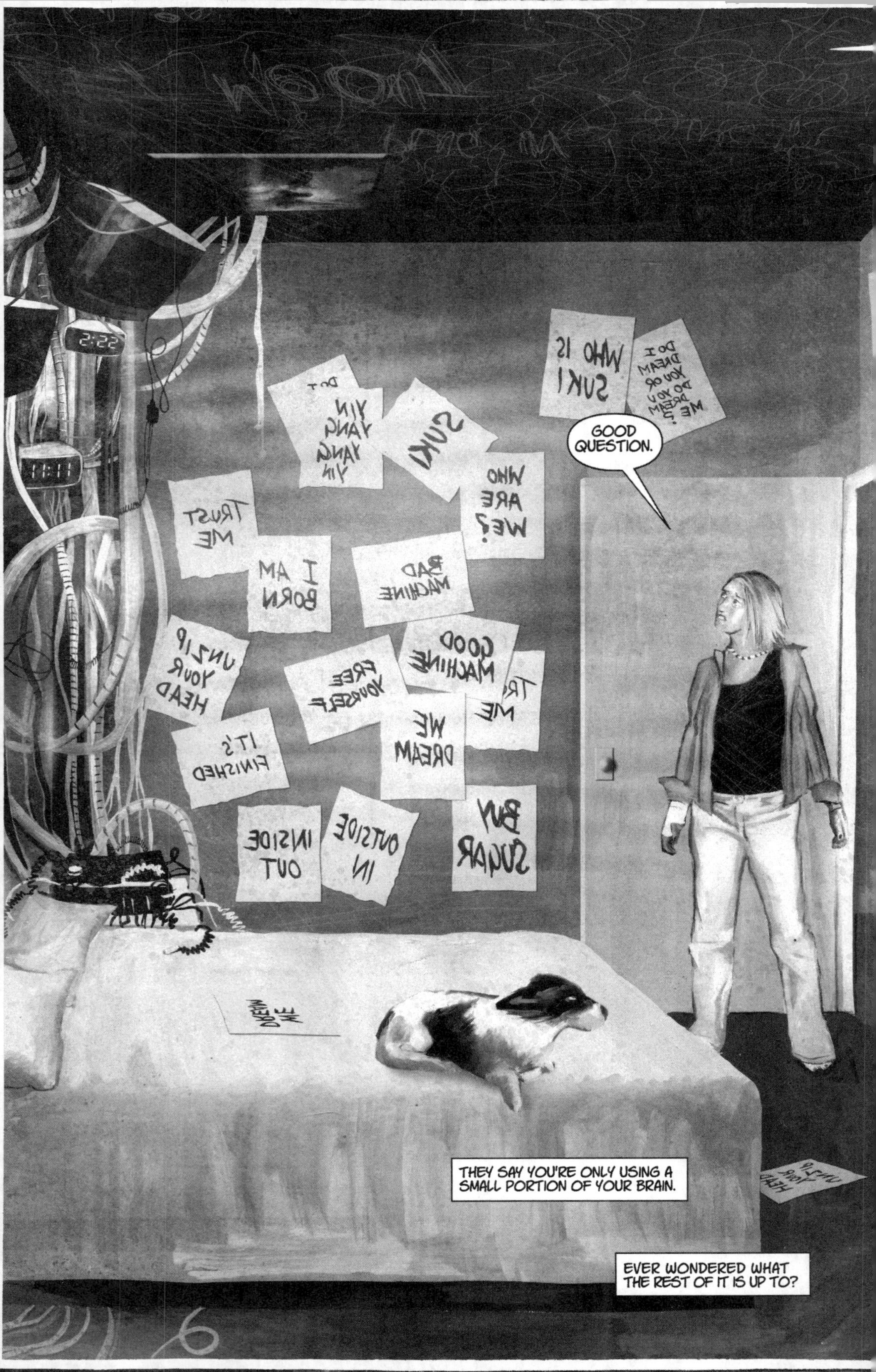
GOOD QUESTION.
THEY SAY YOU'RE ONLY USING A SMALL PORTION OF YOUR BRAIN.
EVER WONDERED WHAT THE REST OF IT IS UP TO?

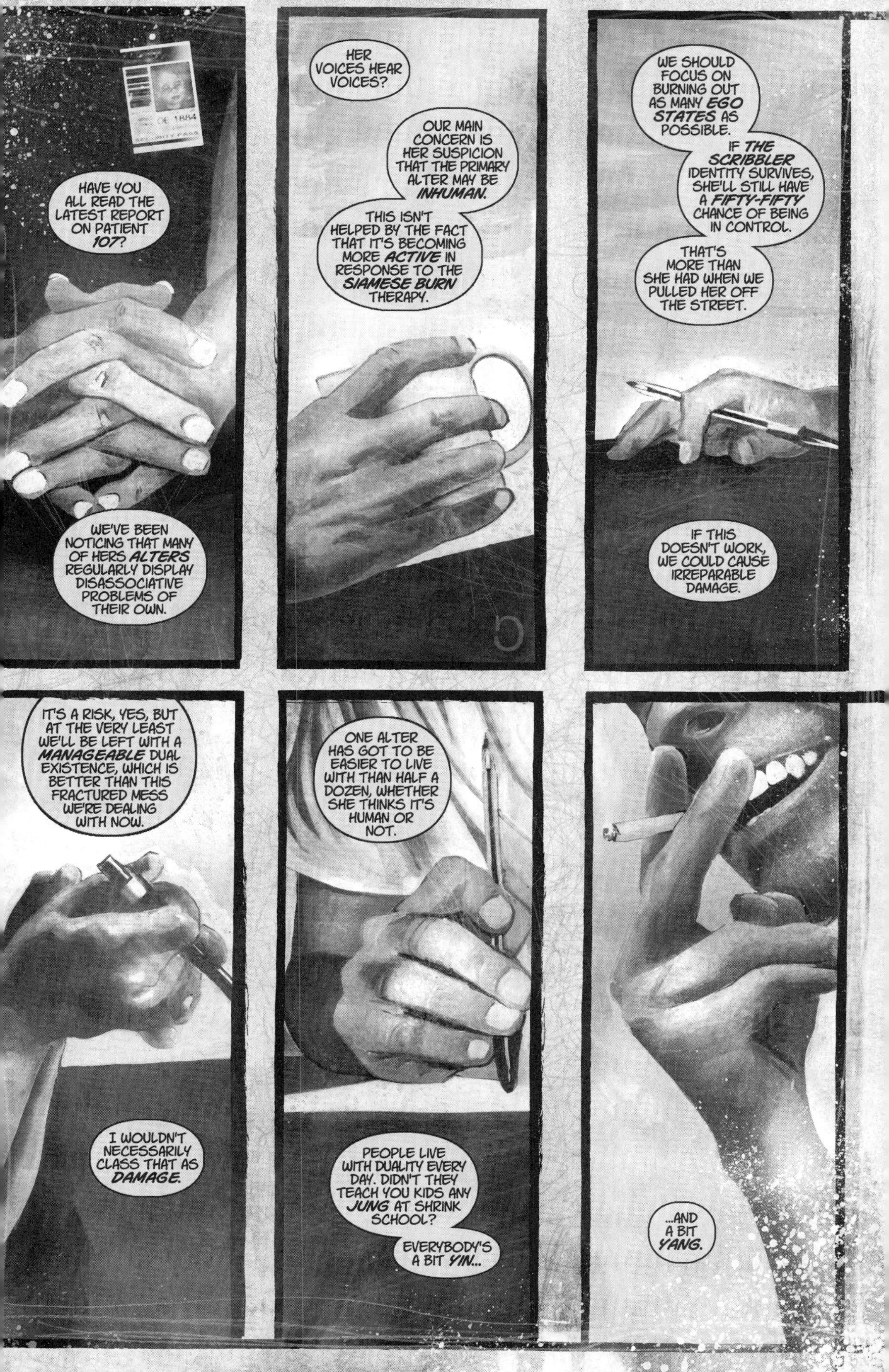
HAVE YOU ALL READ THE LATEST REPORT ON PATIENT 107?
WE'VE BEEN NOTICING THAT MANY OF HERS ALTERS REGULARLY DISPLAY DISASSOCIATIVE PROBLEMS OF THEIR OWN.
HER VOICES HEAR VOICES?
OUR MAIN CONCERN IS HER SUSPICION THAT THE PRIMARY ALTER MAY BE INHUMAN.
THIS ISN'T HELPED BY THE FACT THAT IT'S BECOMING MORE ACTIVE IN RESPONSE TO THE SIAMESE BURN THERAPY.
WE SHOULD FOCUS ON BURNING OUT AS MANY EGO STATES AS POSSIBLE.
IF THE SCRIBBLER IDENTITY SURVIVES, SHE'LL STILL HAVE A FIFTY-FIFTY CHANCE OF BEING IN CONTROL.
THAT'S MORE THAN SHE HAD WHEN WE PULLED HER OFF THE STREET.
IF THIS DOESN'T WORK, WE COULD CAUSE IRREPARABLE DAMAGE.
IT'S A RISK, YES, BUT AT THE VERY LEAST WE'LL BE LEFT WITH A MANAGEABLE DUAL EXISTENCE, WHICH IS BETTER THAN THIS FRACTURED MESS WE'RE DEALING WITH NOW.
I WOULDN'T NECESSARILY CLASS THAT AS DAMAGE.
ONE ALTER HAS GOT TO BE EASIER TO LIVE WITH THAN HALF A DOZEN, WHETHER SHE THINKS IT'S HUMAN OR NOT.
PEOPLE LIVE WITH DUALITY EVERY DAY. DIDN'T THEY TEACH YOU KIDS ANY JUNG AT SHRINK SCHOOL?
EVERYBODY'S A BIT YIN...
...AND A BIT YANG.

IT LOOKS LIKE *TETSUO THE IRON MAN* TOOK A DUMP IN THE MIDDLE OF MY BEDROOM.

ALL THESE WIRES AND CIRCUIT BOARDS, SOME OF THEM BELONGED TO HOGAN'S CAMERA.

HE'S GOING TO BLOW A *FUSE* OF HIS OWN WHEN I SHOW HIM THIS.

YOU WERE SUPPOSED TO BE ON LOOKOUT, YOU LITTLE SHIT.

SO WHAT DID YOU SEE? WAS IT AN ALIEN ABDUCTION? COME ON, YOU CAN TELL ME.

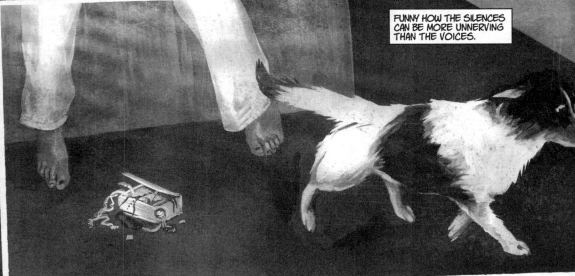

FUNNY HOW THE SILENCES CAN BE MORE UNNERVING THAN THE VOICES.

FINE. JUST PISS OFF AT THE FIRST SIGN OF TROUBLE.

IT'S WHAT YOU'RE GOOD AT.

YEAH, YOU HEARD ME RIGHT.

HOW LONG DID YOU STICK IT OUT WITH *ALICE IN LOOPY-LAND* BEFORE YOU TOOK OFF, HUH?

YOU HAVE NO CONSIDERATION FOR ANYONE BUT YOURSELF. YOU JUST GO WHERE THE FOOD IS.

I SHOULDN'T THINK IT, BUT IT'S TOO LATE. THE IDEA IS ALREADY IN MY HEAD.

NO, NO, NO. *BAD* IDEA. AND IT WOULD BE WRONG. I SHOULD SAY THAT OUT LOUD, JUST SO I HEAR IT FOR MYSELF.

IT WOULD BE WRONG.

WRONGWRONGWRONG.

THEN AGAIN...

...I'M A CRAZY PERSON. THE *VOICES* MAKE ME DO CRAZY THINGS.

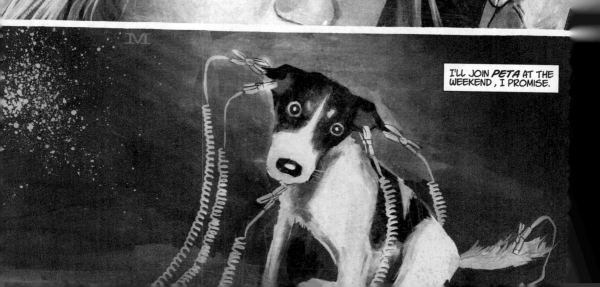

I'LL JOIN *PETA* AT THE WEEKEND, I PROMISE.

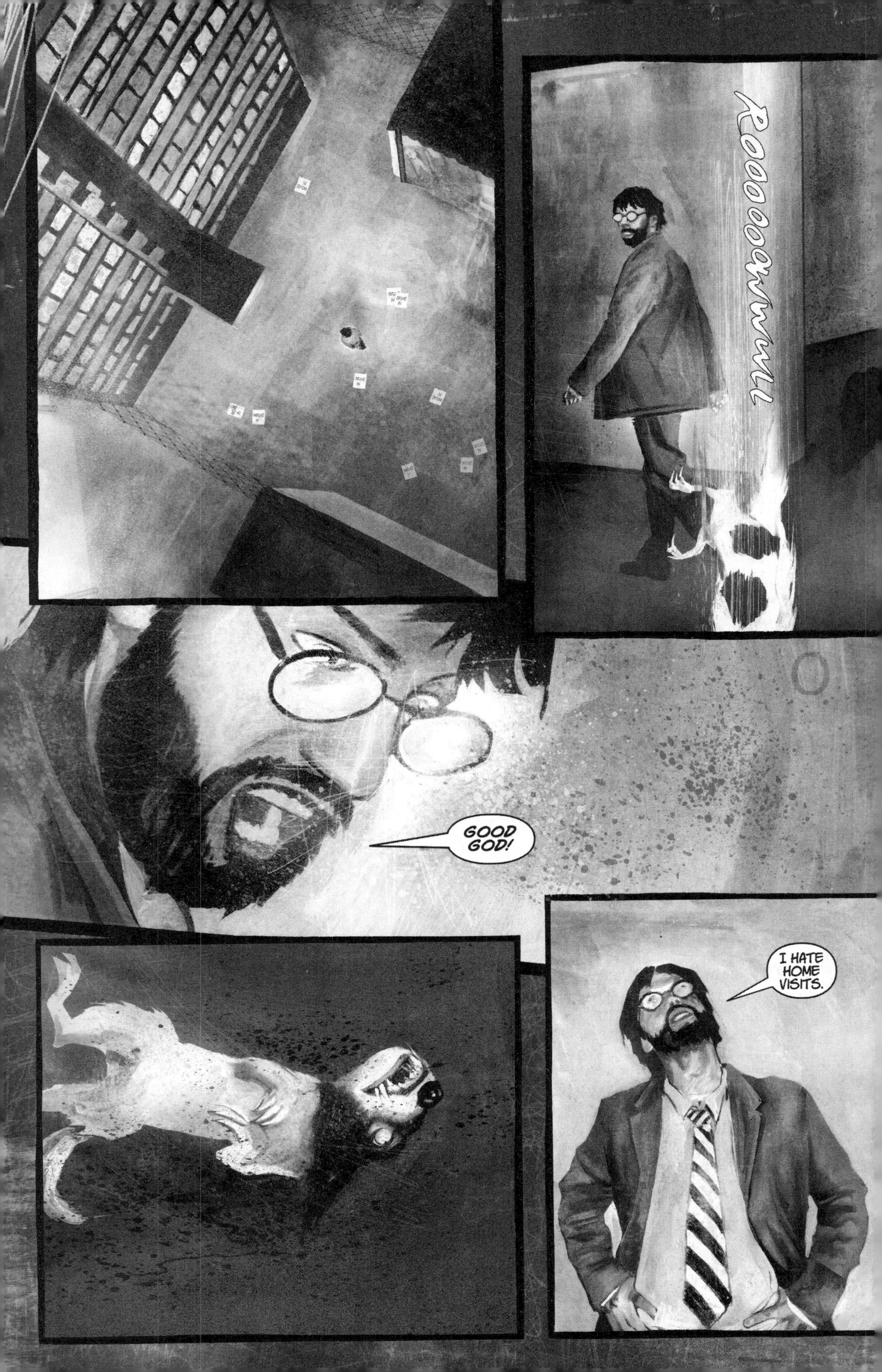
ROOOOOWWLL
GOOD GOD!
I HATE HOME VISITS.

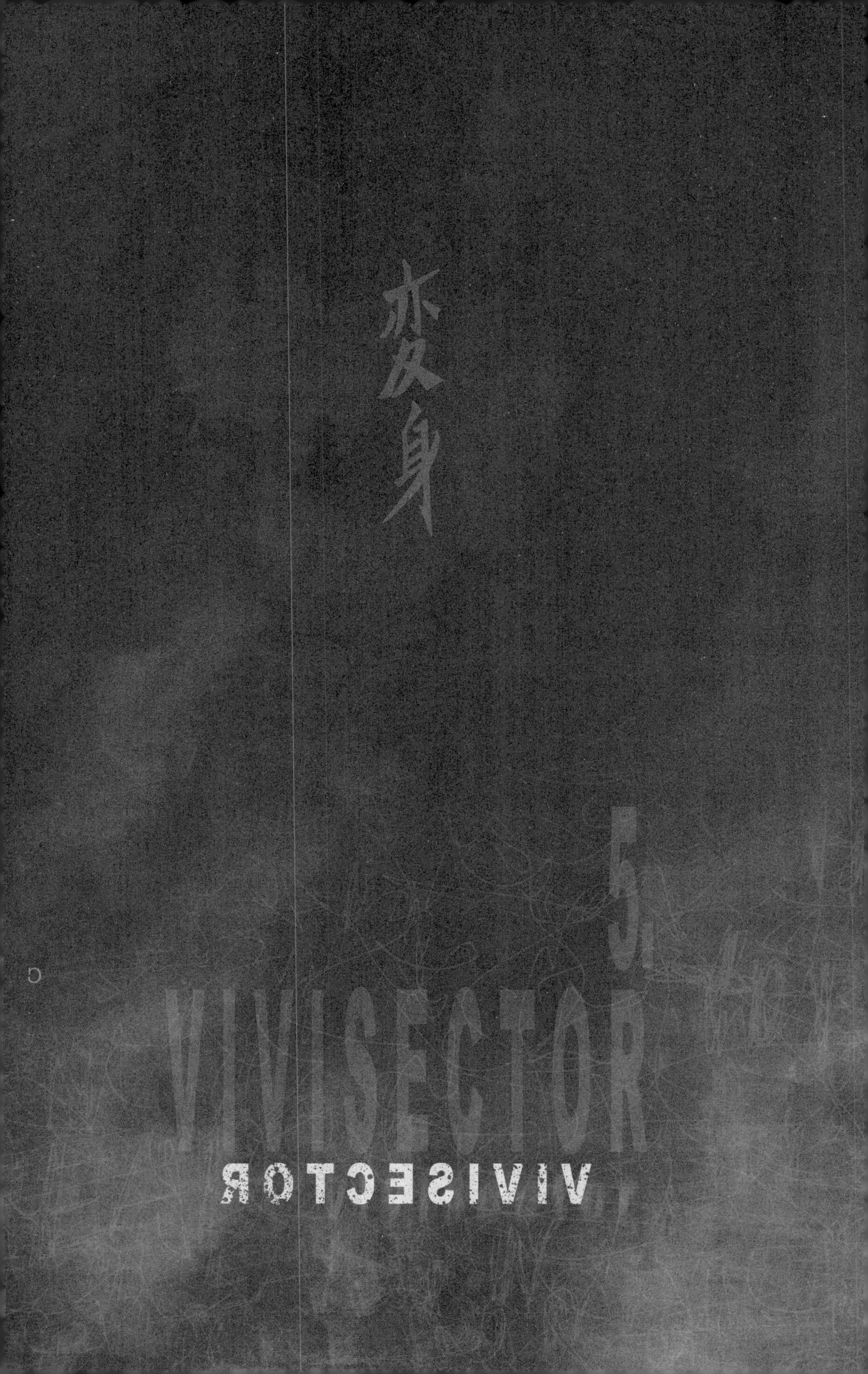
変身
5
VIVISECTOR
VIVISECTOR

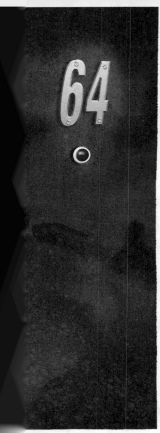

64

DAMN.

DOCTOR SINCLAIR. I THOUGHT YOU WERE COMING ON FRIDAY.

IN THE LIGHT OF THE CURRENT SUICIDE RATE AT THIS BLOCK, I THOUGHT IT MIGHT BE PRUDENT TO CHECK UP ON YOU.

DO YOU OWN A DOG?

NO. WHY? WHO TOLD YOU THAT?

IT DOESN'T MATTER. I SEE YOU'VE REDECORATED THE PLACE.

YOU'RE STILL ON THE MACHINE, AREN'T YOU? YOU KNOW YOU CAN'T AFFORD TO MISS A SESSION.

DOG FOOD

RELAX, DOC.

I'M DOING EVERYTHING BY THE BOOK.

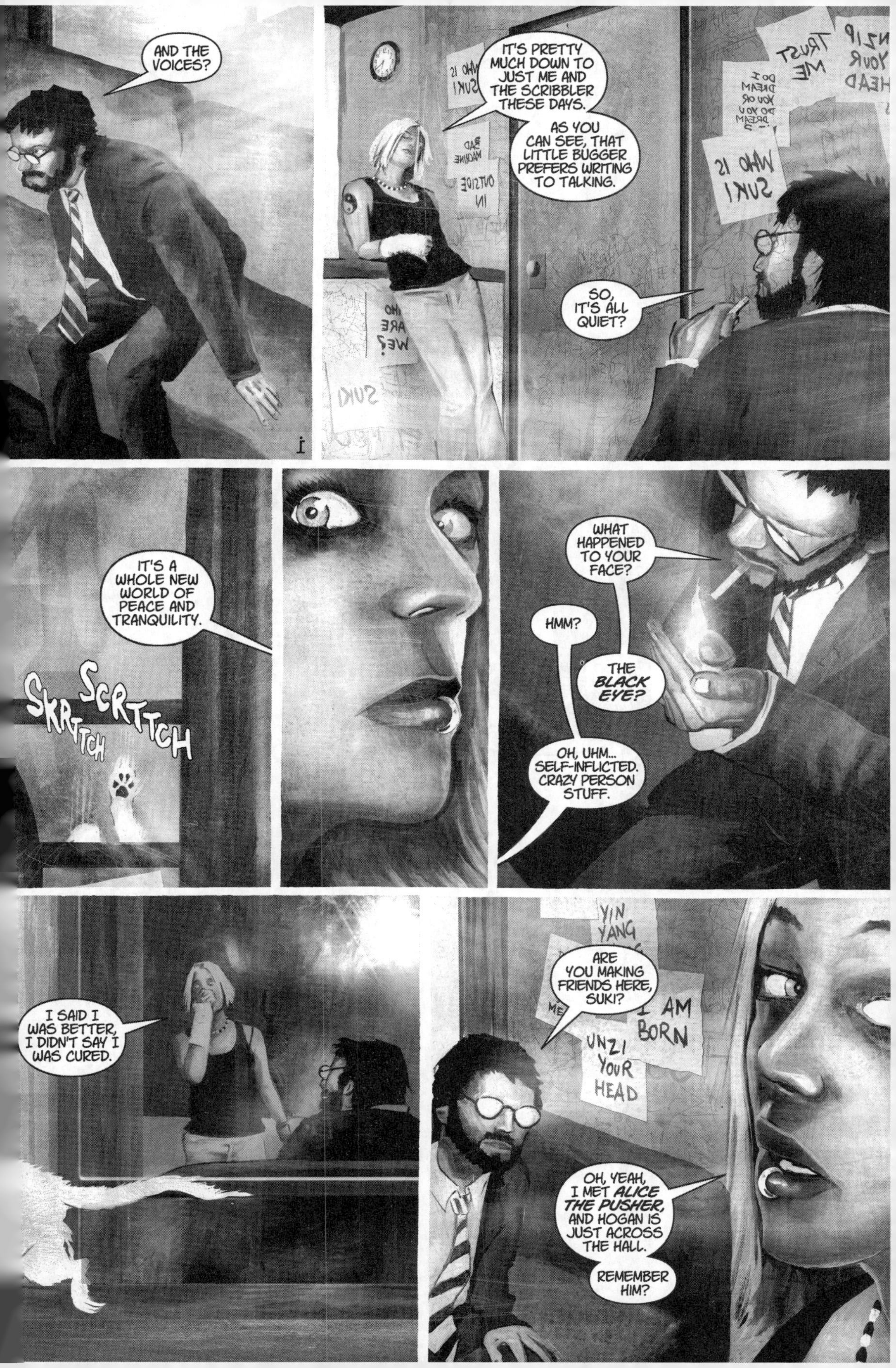
AND THE VOICES?
IT'S PRETTY MUCH DOWN TO JUST ME AND THE SCRIBBLER THESE DAYS.
AS YOU CAN SEE, THAT LITTLE BUGGER PREFERS WRITING TO TALKING.
TRUST ME
SO, IT'S ALL QUIET?
IT'S A WHOLE NEW WORLD OF PEACE AND TRANQUILITY.
SCRTTTCH
SKRTTCH
WHAT HAPPENED TO YOUR FACE?
HMM?
THE BLACK EYE?
OH, UHM... SELF-INFLICTED. CRAZY PERSON STUFF.
I SAID I WAS BETTER, I DIDN'T SAY I WAS CURED.
YIN YANG
ARE YOU MAKING FRIENDS HERE, SUKI?
I AM BORN
UNZI YOUR HEAD
OH, YEAH, I MET ALICE THE PUSHER, AND HOGAN IS JUST ACROSS THE HALL.
REMEMBER HIM?

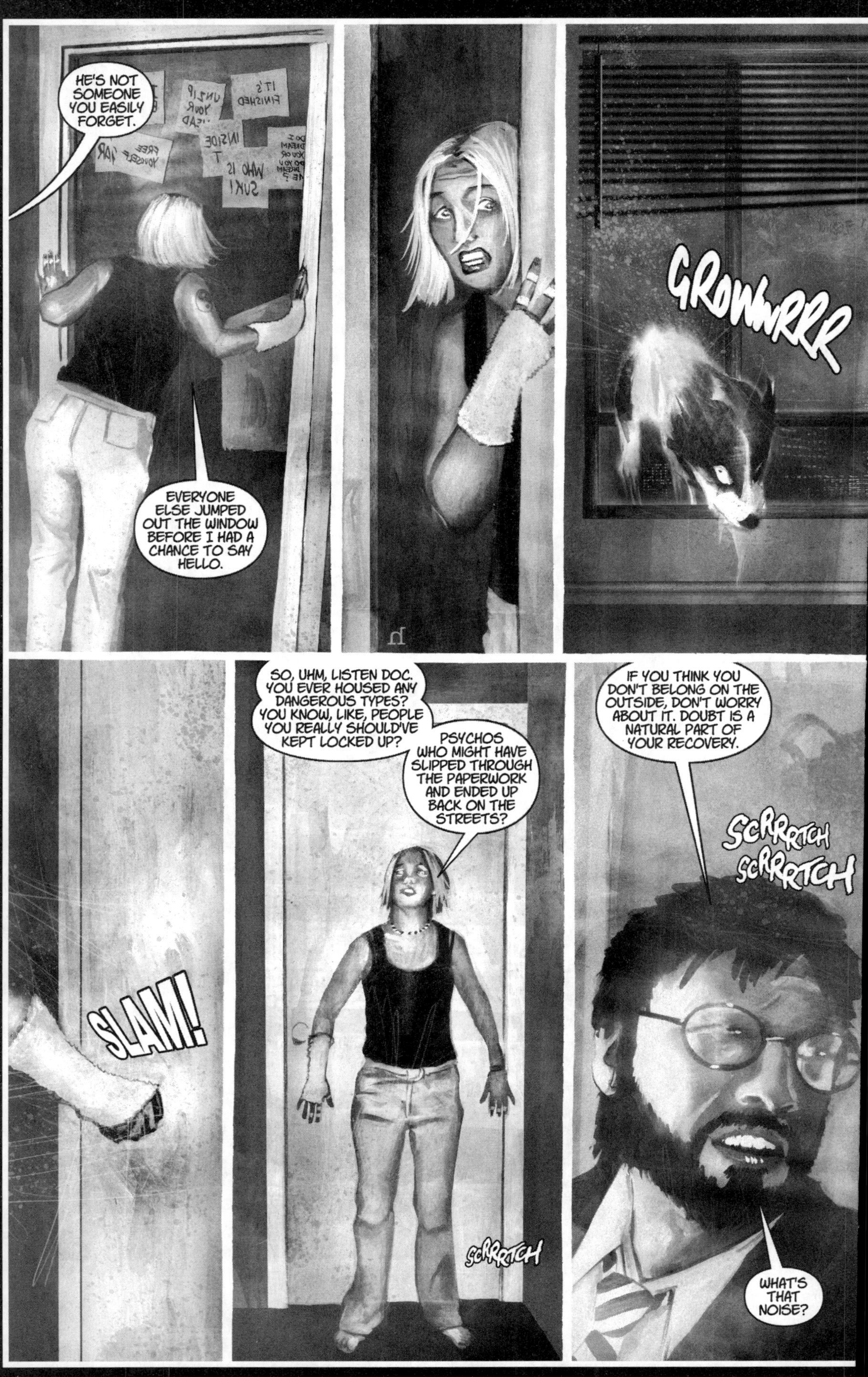
HE'S NOT SOMEONE YOU EASILY FORGET.
EVERYONE ELSE JUMPED OUT THE WINDOW BEFORE I HAD A CHANCE TO SAY HELLO.
GROWWRRR
SLAM!
SO, UHM, LISTEN DOC. YOU EVER HOUSED ANY DANGEROUS TYPES? YOU KNOW, LIKE, PEOPLE YOU REALLY SHOULD'VE KEPT LOCKED UP?
PSYCHOS WHO MIGHT HAVE SLIPPED THROUGH THE PAPERWORK AND ENDED UP BACK ON THE STREETS?
SCRRRTCH
IF YOU THINK YOU DON'T BELONG ON THE OUTSIDE, DON'T WORRY ABOUT IT. DOUBT IS A NATURAL PART OF YOUR RECOVERY.
SCRRRTCH
SCRRRTCH
WHAT'S THAT NOISE?

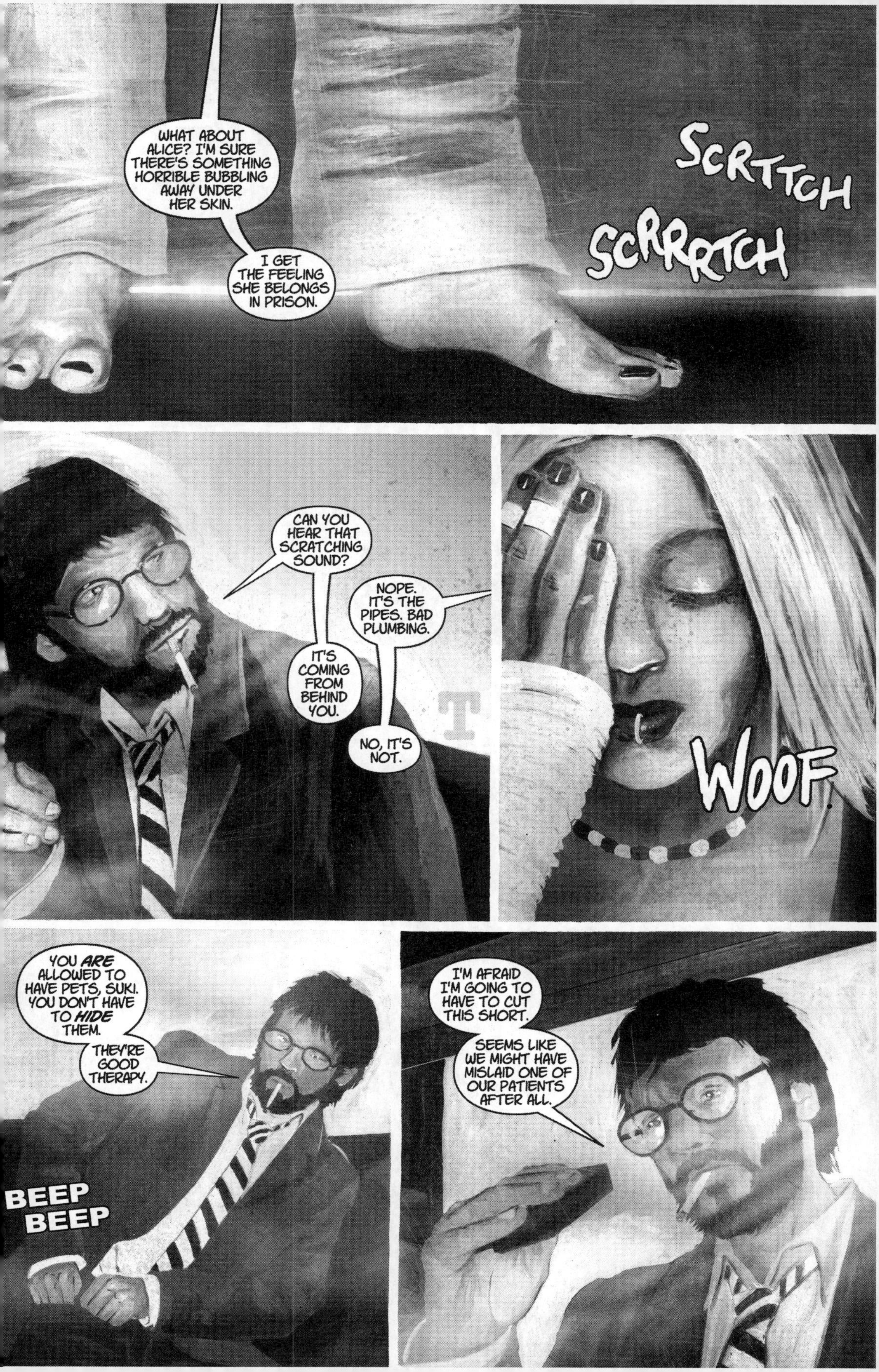
WHAT ABOUT ALICE? I'M SURE THERE'S SOMETHING HORRIBLE BUBBLING AWAY UNDER HER SKIN.
I GET THE FEELING SHE BELONGS IN PRISON.
SCRTTCH
SCRRRTCH
CAN YOU HEAR THAT SCRATCHING SOUND?
NOPE. IT'S THE PIPES. BAD PLUMBING.
IT'S COMING FROM BEHIND YOU.
NO, IT'S NOT.
WOOF
YOU *ARE* ALLOWED TO HAVE PETS, SUKI. YOU DON'T HAVE TO *HIDE* THEM.
THEY'RE GOOD THERAPY.
BEEP BEEP
I'M AFRAID I'M GOING TO HAVE TO CUT THIS SHORT.
SEEMS LIKE WE MIGHT HAVE MISLAID ONE OF OUR PATIENTS AFTER ALL.

YOU'RE KIDDING ME, RIGHT?

THAT'S ALICE'S DOG?

AND YOU'RE SAYING THAT *THIS* IS WHAT HAPPENED TO YOU?

I'M JUST TELLING YOU I'VE GOT *MISSING TIME.*

I'M NOT SAYING I'M THE SODDING *WOLFMAN* OR ANYTHING.

HOW SCARED DO YOU THINK I SHOULD BE?

I DON'T KNOW. HAVE YOU FELT THE URGE TO CHEW FURNITURE OR SNIFF ANYONE ELSE'S ARSE LATELY?

HOW IS THAT HELPING?

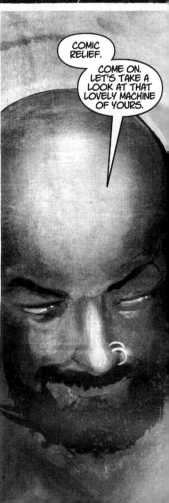

COMIC RELIEF.

COME ON. LET'S TAKE A LOOK AT THAT LOVELY MACHINE OF YOURS.

自由

6. UNZIPPED

UNZIPPED

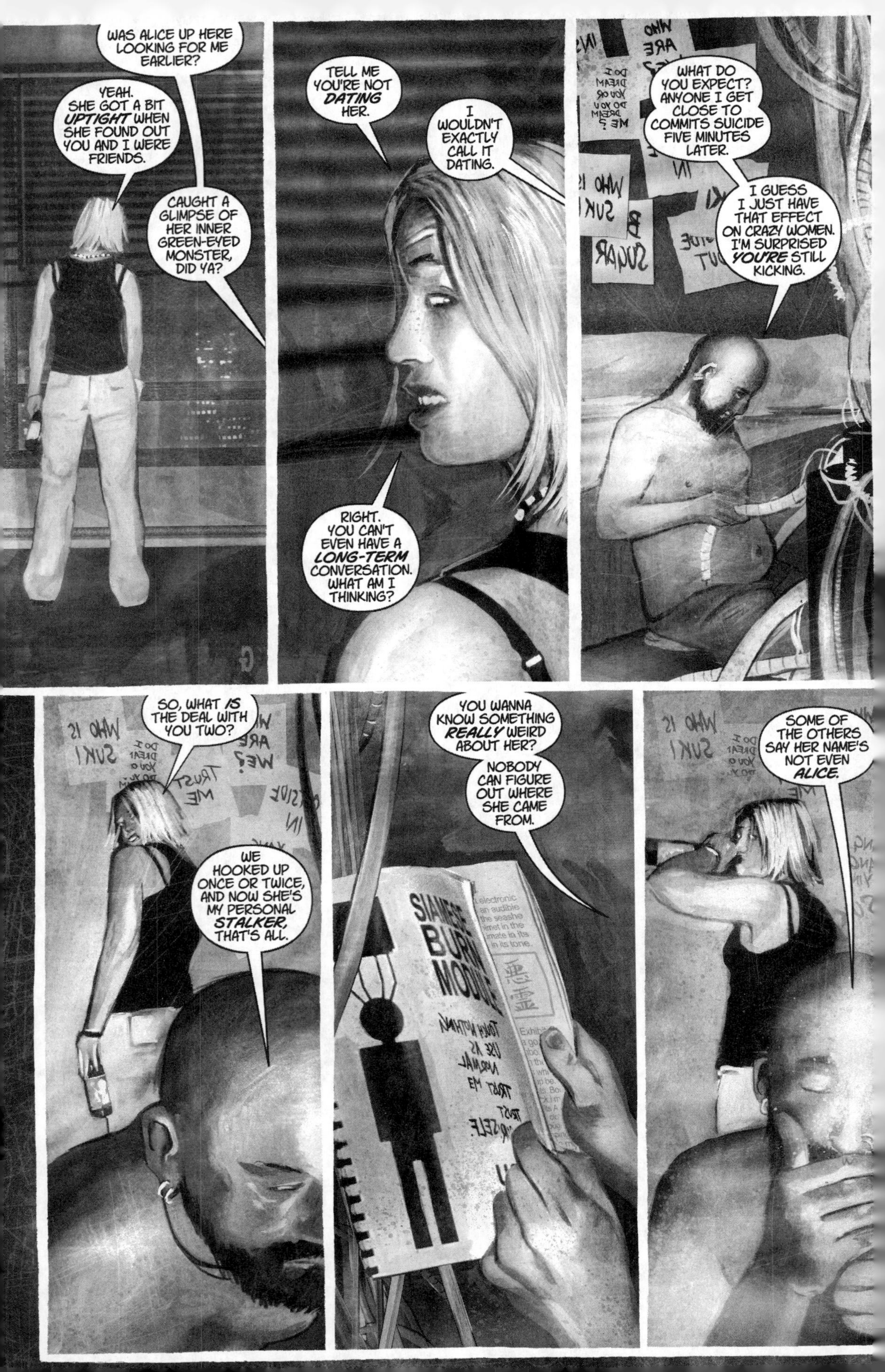
WAS ALICE UP HERE LOOKING FOR ME EARLIER?
YEAH. SHE GOT A BIT UPTIGHT WHEN SHE FOUND OUT YOU AND I WERE FRIENDS.
CAUGHT A GLIMPSE OF HER INNER GREEN-EYED MONSTER, DID YA?
TELL ME YOU'RE NOT DATING HER.
I WOULDN'T EXACTLY CALL IT DATING.
RIGHT. YOU CAN'T EVEN HAVE A LONG-TERM CONVERSATION. WHAT AM I THINKING?
WHO ARE WE?
DO I DREAM YOU OR DO YOU DREAM ME?
WHO IS SUKI
SUGAR
WHAT DO YOU EXPECT? ANYONE I GET CLOSE TO COMMITS SUICIDE FIVE MINUTES LATER.
I GUESS I JUST HAVE THAT EFFECT ON CRAZY WOMEN. I'M SURPRISED YOU'RE STILL KICKING.
SO, WHAT IS THE DEAL WITH YOU TWO?
WHO IS SUKI
WHO ARE WE?
TRUST ME
WE HOOKED UP ONCE OR TWICE, AND NOW SHE'S MY PERSONAL STALKER, THAT'S ALL.
YOU WANNA KNOW SOMETHING REALLY WEIRD ABOUT HER?
NOBODY CAN FIGURE OUT WHERE SHE CAME FROM.
SIAMESE BURN MODULE
TRUST ME
SOME OF THE OTHERS SAY HER NAME'S NOT EVEN ALICE.

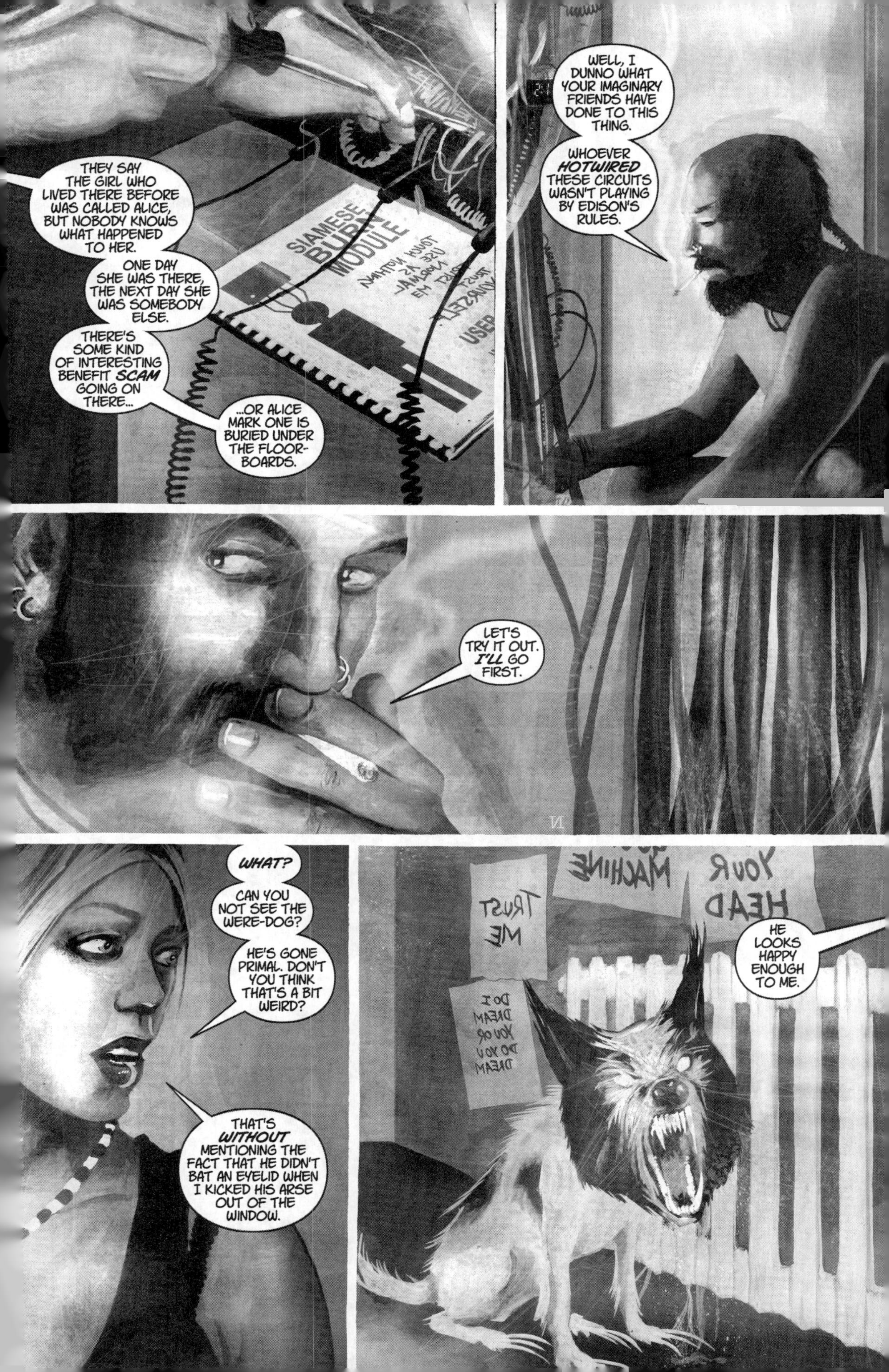
SIAMESE BURN MODULE
THEY SAY THE GIRL WHO LIVED THERE BEFORE WAS CALLED ALICE, BUT NOBODY KNOWS WHAT HAPPENED TO HER.
ONE DAY SHE WAS THERE, THE NEXT DAY SHE WAS SOMEBODY ELSE.
THERE'S SOME KIND OF INTERESTING BENEFIT *SCAM* GOING ON THERE...
...OR ALICE MARK ONE IS BURIED UNDER THE FLOOR-BOARDS.
WELL, I DUNNO WHAT YOUR IMAGINARY FRIENDS HAVE DONE TO THIS THING.
WHOEVER ***HOTWIRED*** THESE CIRCUITS WASN'T PLAYING BY EDISON'S RULES.
LET'S TRY IT OUT. ***I'LL*** GO FIRST.
WHAT?
CAN YOU NOT SEE THE WERE-DOG?
HE'S GONE PRIMAL. DON'T YOU THINK THAT'S A BIT WEIRD?
THAT'S ***WITHOUT*** MENTIONING THE FACT THAT HE DIDN'T BAT AN EYELID WHEN I KICKED HIS ARSE OUT OF THE WINDOW.
HE LOOKS HAPPY ENOUGH TO ME.

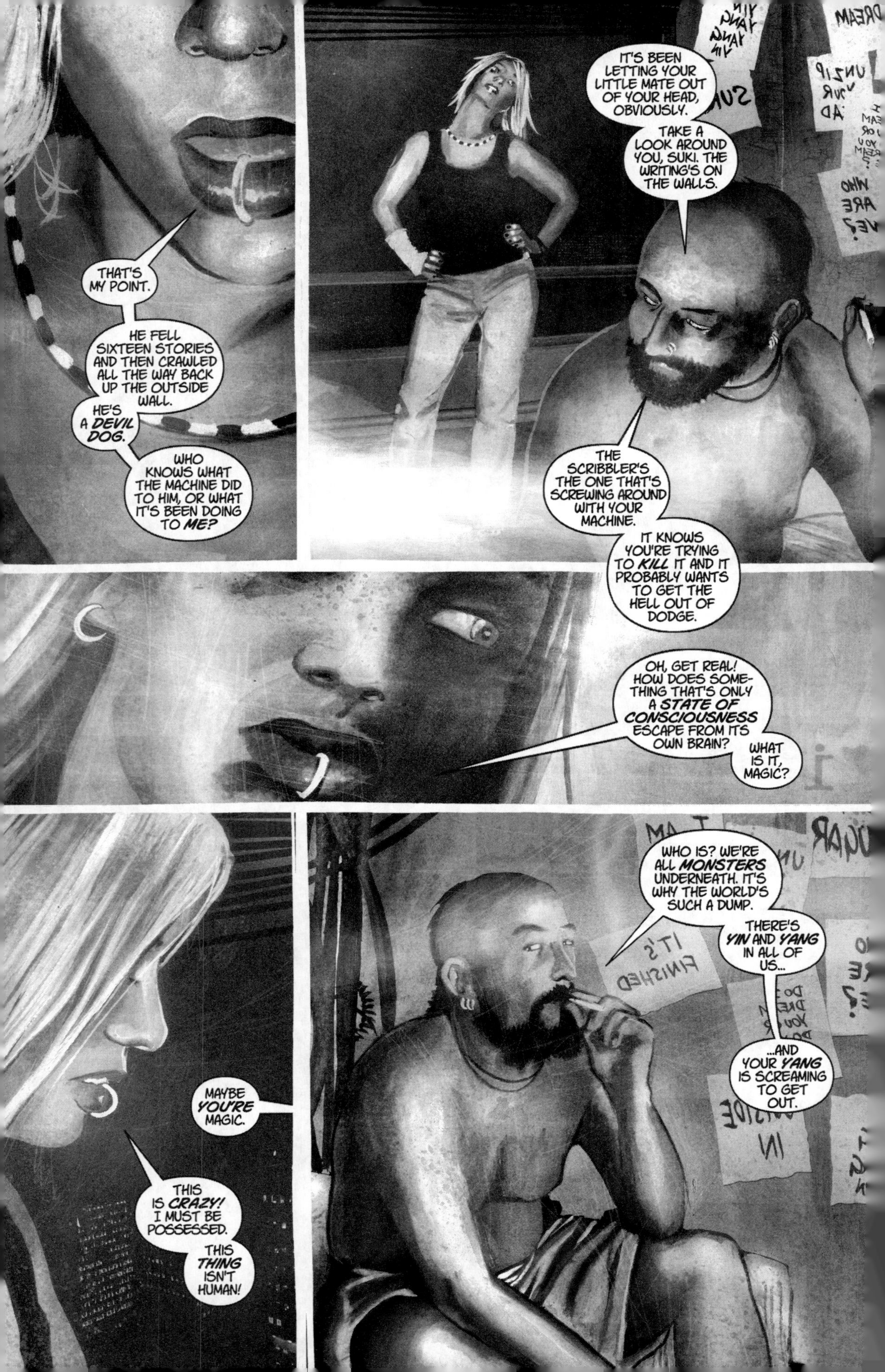
THAT'S MY POINT.
HE FELL SIXTEEN STORIES AND THEN CRAWLED ALL THE WAY BACK UP THE OUTSIDE WALL.
HE'S A DEVIL DOG.
WHO KNOWS WHAT THE MACHINE DID TO HIM, OR WHAT IT'S BEEN DOING TO ME?
IT'S BEEN LETTING YOUR LITTLE MATE OUT OF YOUR HEAD, OBVIOUSLY.
TAKE A LOOK AROUND YOU, SUKI. THE WRITING'S ON THE WALLS.
THE SCRIBBLER'S THE ONE THAT'S SCREWING AROUND WITH YOUR MACHINE.
IT KNOWS YOU'RE TRYING TO KILL IT AND IT PROBABLY WANTS TO GET THE HELL OUT OF DODGE.
OH, GET REAL! HOW DOES SOMETHING THAT'S ONLY A STATE OF CONSCIOUSNESS ESCAPE FROM ITS OWN BRAIN?
WHAT IS IT, MAGIC?
WHO IS? WE'RE ALL MONSTERS UNDERNEATH. IT'S WHY THE WORLD'S SUCH A DUMP.
THERE'S YIN AND YANG IN ALL OF US...
...AND YOUR YANG IS SCREAMING TO GET OUT.
MAYBE YOU'RE MAGIC.
THIS IS CRAZY! I MUST BE POSSESSED.
THIS THING ISN'T HUMAN!
IT'S FINISHED

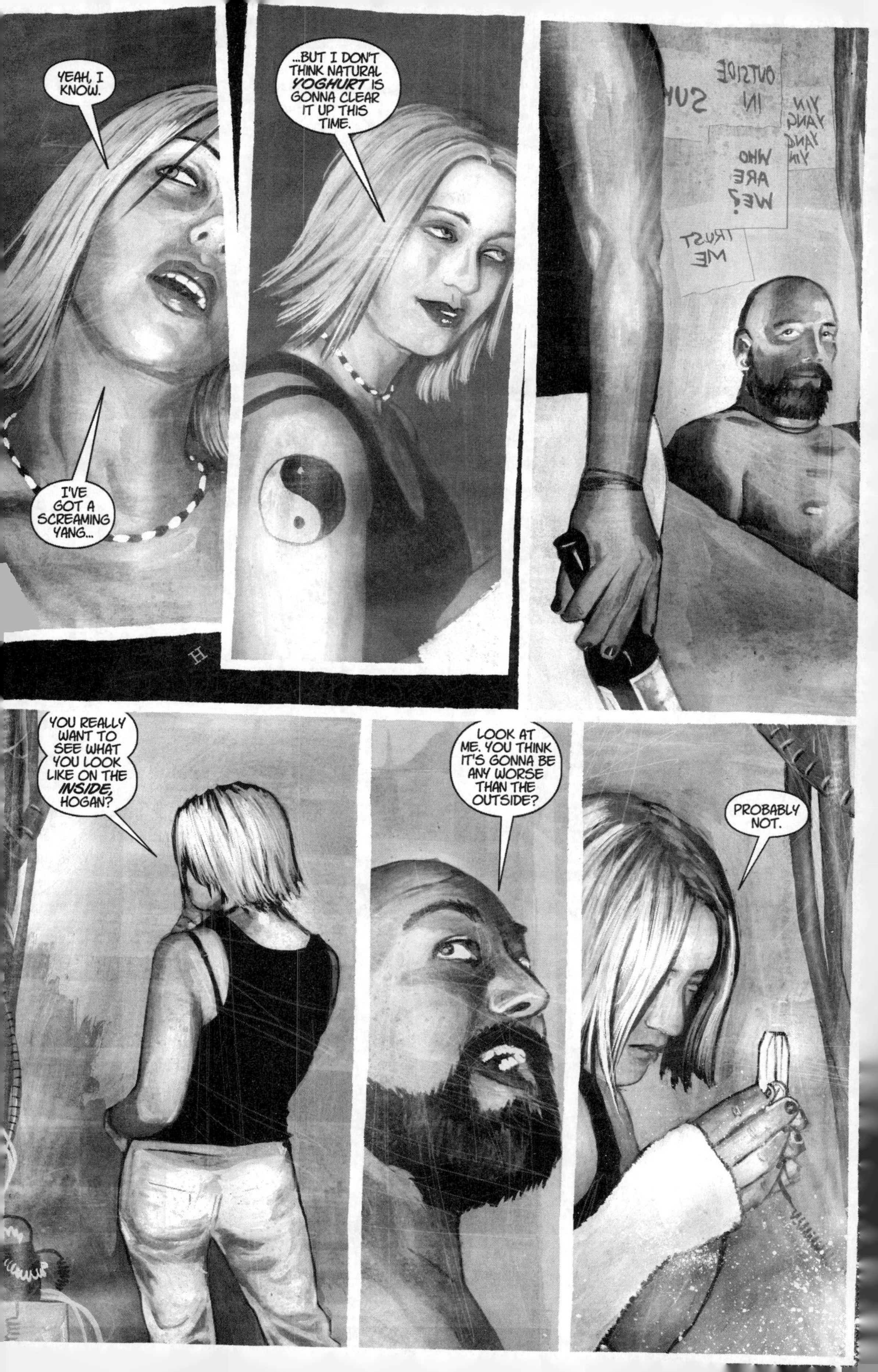
YEAH, I KNOW.
I'VE GOT A SCREAMING YANG...
...BUT I DON'T THINK NATURAL YOGHURT IS GONNA CLEAR IT UP THIS TIME.
YOU REALLY WANT TO SEE WHAT YOU LOOK LIKE ON THE INSIDE, HOGAN?
LOOK AT ME. YOU THINK IT'S GONNA BE ANY WORSE THAN THE OUTSIDE?
PROBABLY NOT.

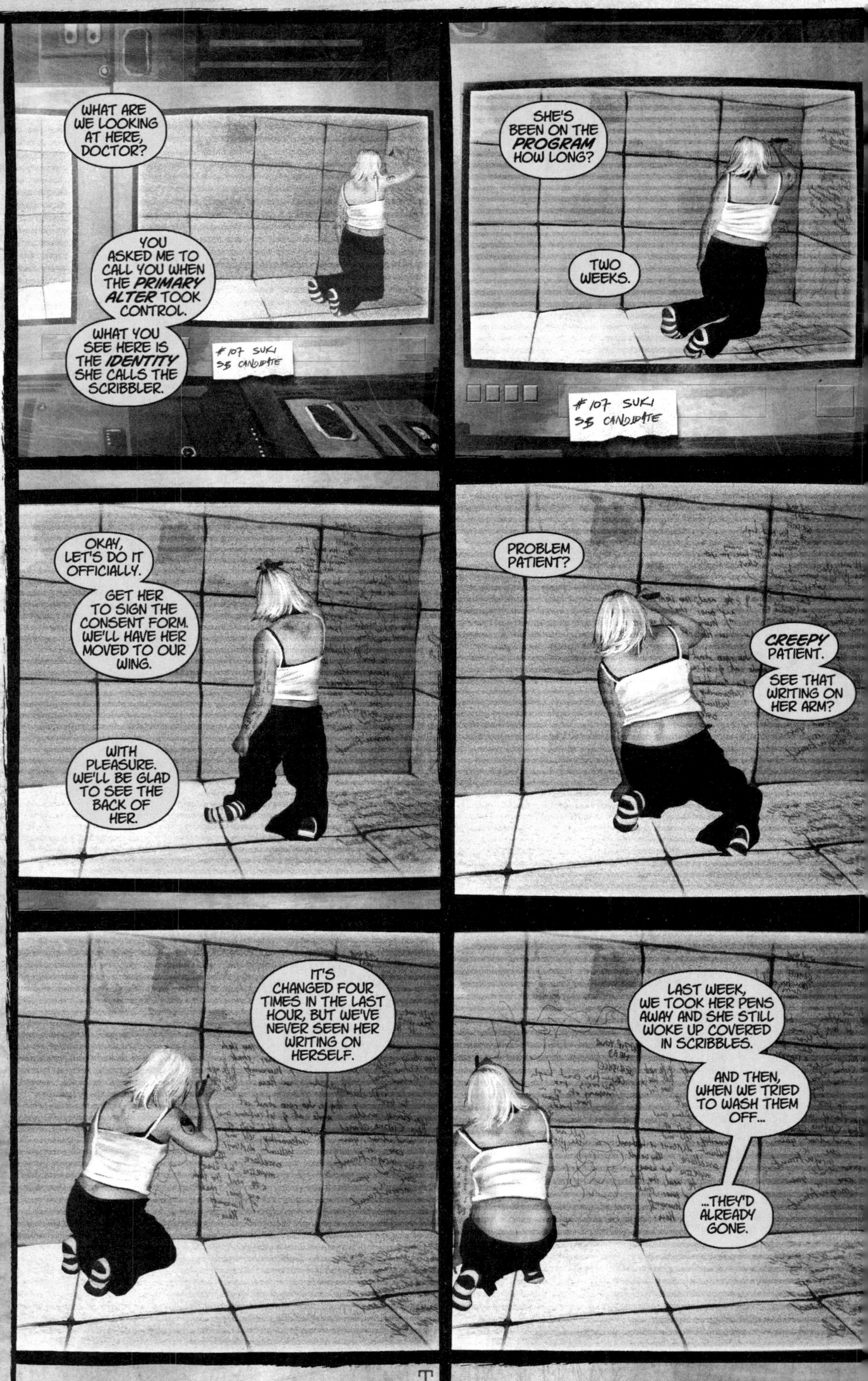
WHAT ARE WE LOOKING AT HERE, DOCTOR?
YOU ASKED ME TO CALL YOU WHEN THE PRIMARY ALTER TOOK CONTROL.
WHAT YOU SEE HERE IS THE IDENTITY SHE CALLS THE SCRIBBLER.
#107 SUKI SB CANDIDATE
SHE'S BEEN ON THE PROGRAM HOW LONG?
TWO WEEKS.
#107 SUKI SB CANDIDATE
OKAY, LET'S DO IT OFFICIALLY.
GET HER TO SIGN THE CONSENT FORM. WE'LL HAVE HER MOVED TO OUR WING.
WITH PLEASURE. WE'LL BE GLAD TO SEE THE BACK OF HER.
PROBLEM PATIENT?
CREEPY PATIENT.
SEE THAT WRITING ON HER ARM?
IT'S CHANGED FOUR TIMES IN THE LAST HOUR, BUT WE'VE NEVER SEEN HER WRITING ON HERSELF.
LAST WEEK, WE TOOK HER PENS AWAY AND SHE STILL WOKE UP COVERED IN SCRIBBLES.
AND THEN, WHEN WE TRIED TO WASH THEM OFF...
...THEY'D ALREADY GONE.

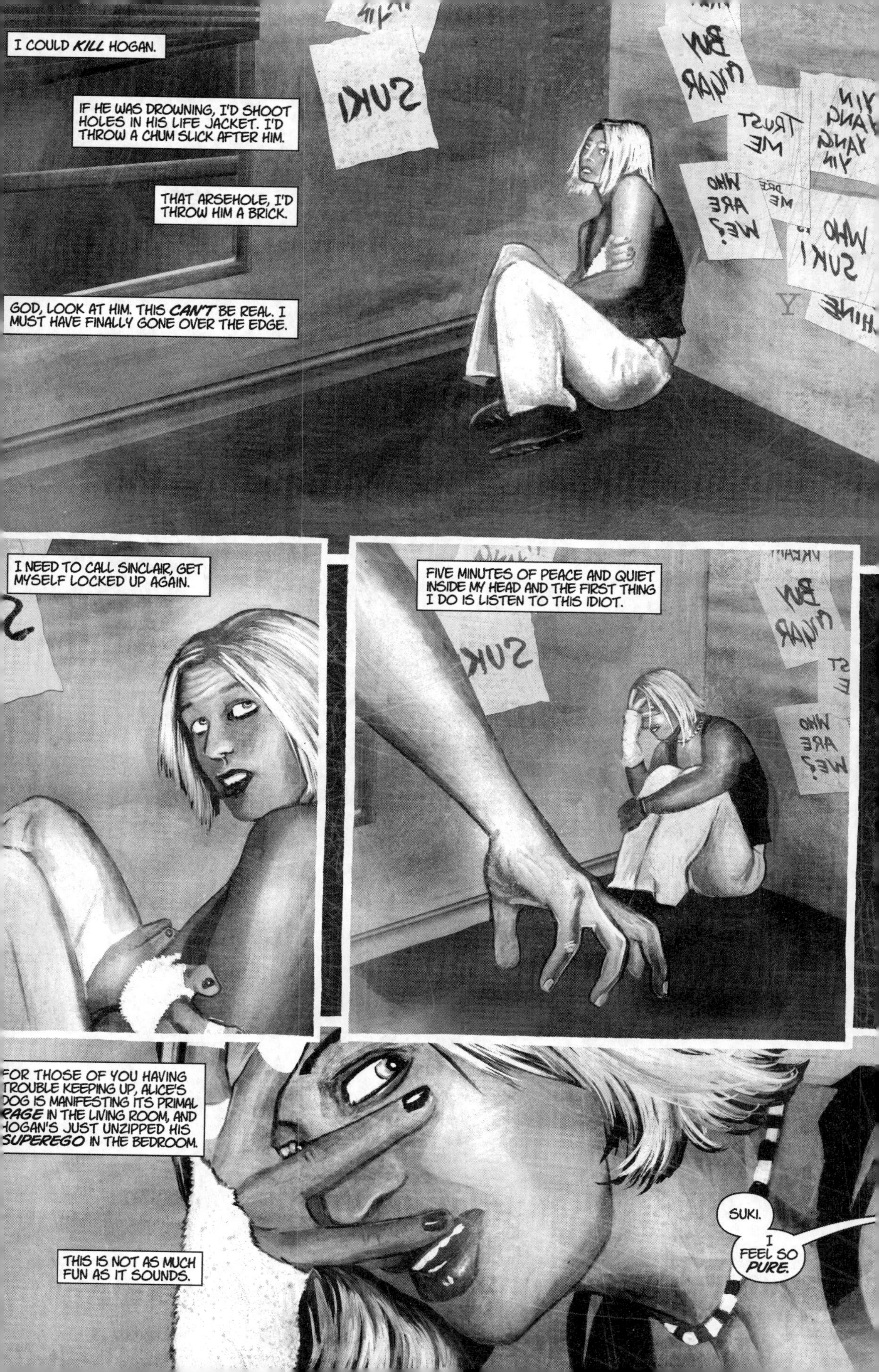
I COULD **KILL** HOGAN.
IF HE WAS DROWNING, I'D SHOOT HOLES IN HIS LIFE JACKET. I'D THROW A CHUM SLICK AFTER HIM.
THAT ARSEHOLE, I'D THROW HIM A BRICK.
GOD, LOOK AT HIM. THIS ***CAN'T*** BE REAL. I MUST HAVE FINALLY GONE OVER THE EDGE.
I NEED TO CALL SINCLAIR, GET MYSELF LOCKED UP AGAIN.
FIVE MINUTES OF PEACE AND QUIET INSIDE MY HEAD AND THE FIRST THING I DO IS LISTEN TO THIS IDIOT.
FOR THOSE OF YOU HAVING TROUBLE KEEPING UP, ALICE'S DOG IS MANIFESTING ITS PRIMAL ***RAGE*** IN THE LIVING ROOM, AND HOGAN'S JUST UNZIPPED HIS ***SUPEREGO*** IN THE BEDROOM.
THIS IS NOT AS MUCH FUN AS IT SOUNDS.
SUKI.
I FEEL SO ***PURE***.

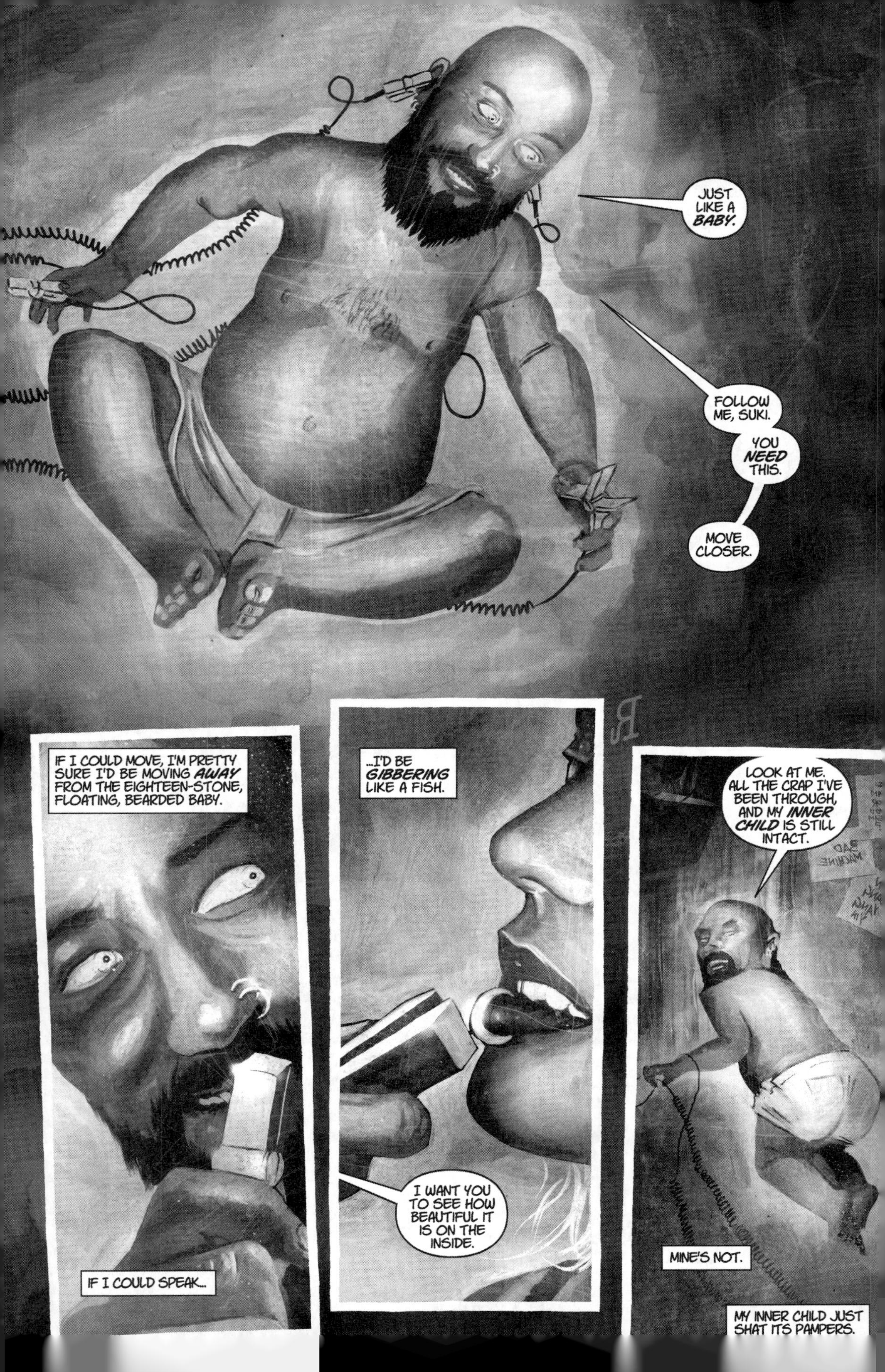
JUST LIKE A BABY.
FOLLOW ME, SUKI.
YOU NEED THIS.
MOVE CLOSER.
IF I COULD MOVE, I'M PRETTY SURE I'D BE MOVING AWAY FROM THE EIGHTEEN-STONE, FLOATING, BEARDED BABY.
IF I COULD SPEAK...
...I'D BE GIBBERING LIKE A FISH.
I WANT YOU TO SEE HOW BEAUTIFUL IT IS ON THE INSIDE.
LOOK AT ME. ALL THE CRAP I'VE BEEN THROUGH, AND MY INNER CHILD IS STILL INTACT.
MINE'S NOT.
MY INNER CHILD JUST SHAT ITS PAMPERS.

DON'T BE AFRAID OF THE SCRIBBLER, SUKI.
IT'S INSIDE YOU.
IT IS YOU.
YOU HAVE TO LET YOURSELF BREATHE.
I FINALLY FIND MY VOICE...
...AND THE BLOODY THING STABS ME RIGHT IN THE BACK.
DO IT.
EXIT SUKI...
CLICK!

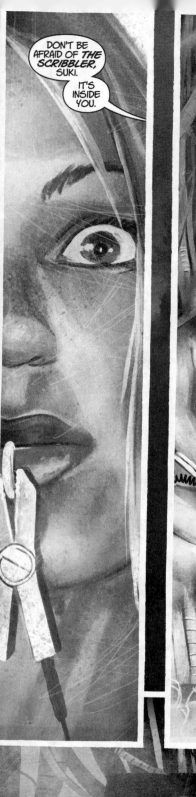

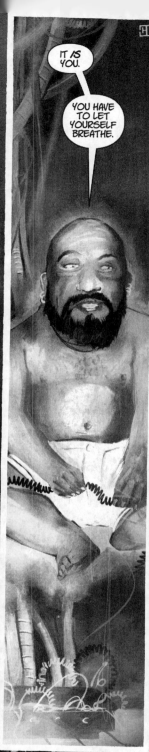

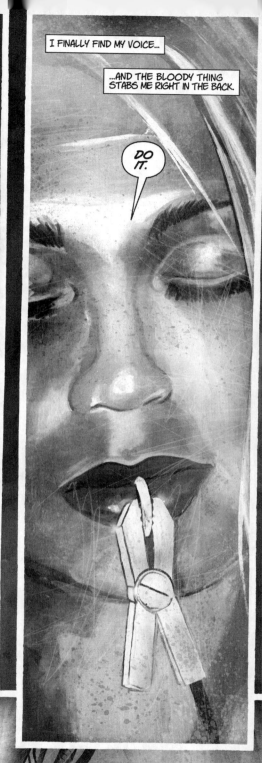

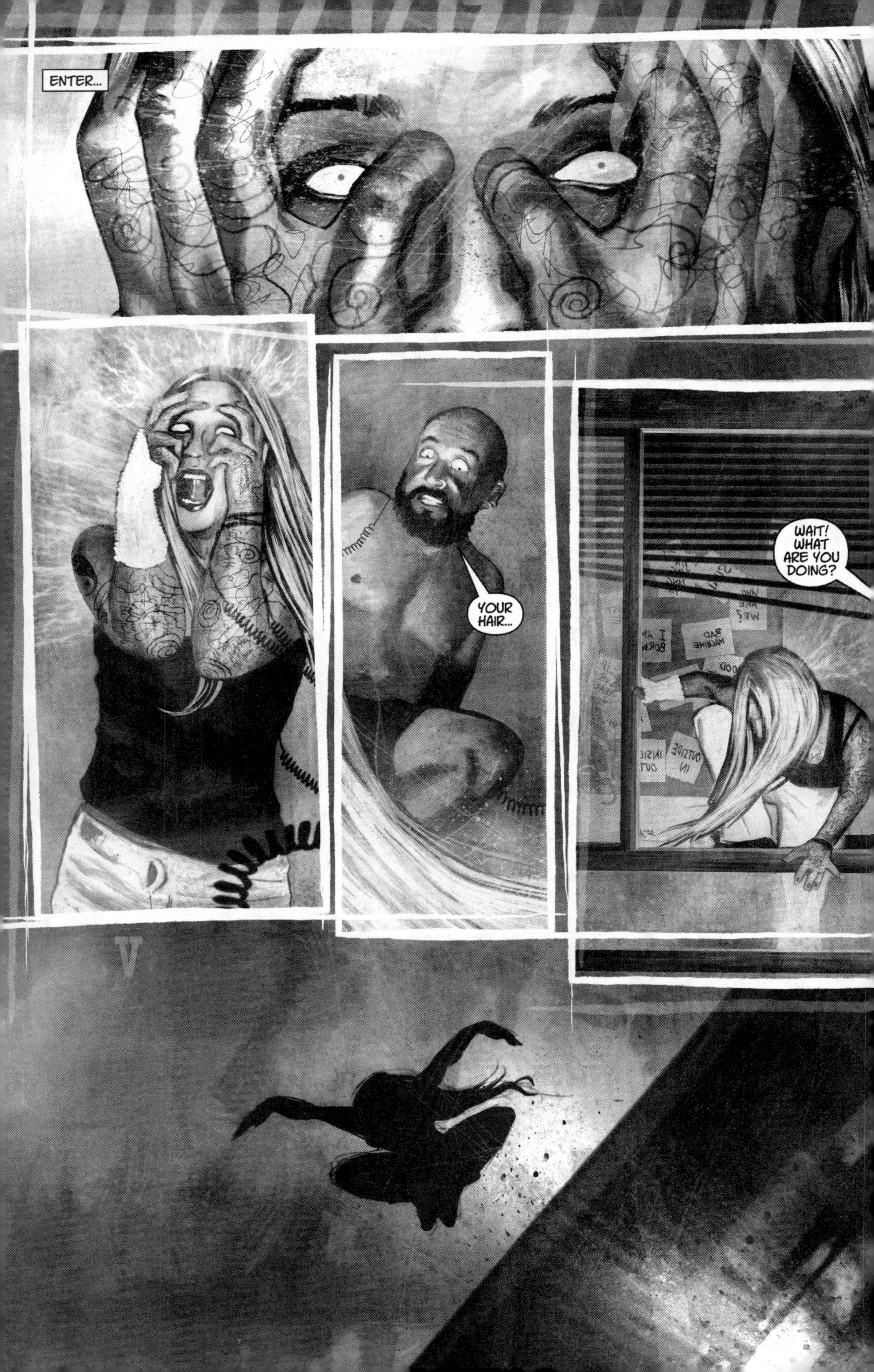
ENTER...
YOUR HAIR...
WAIT! WHAT ARE YOU DOING?

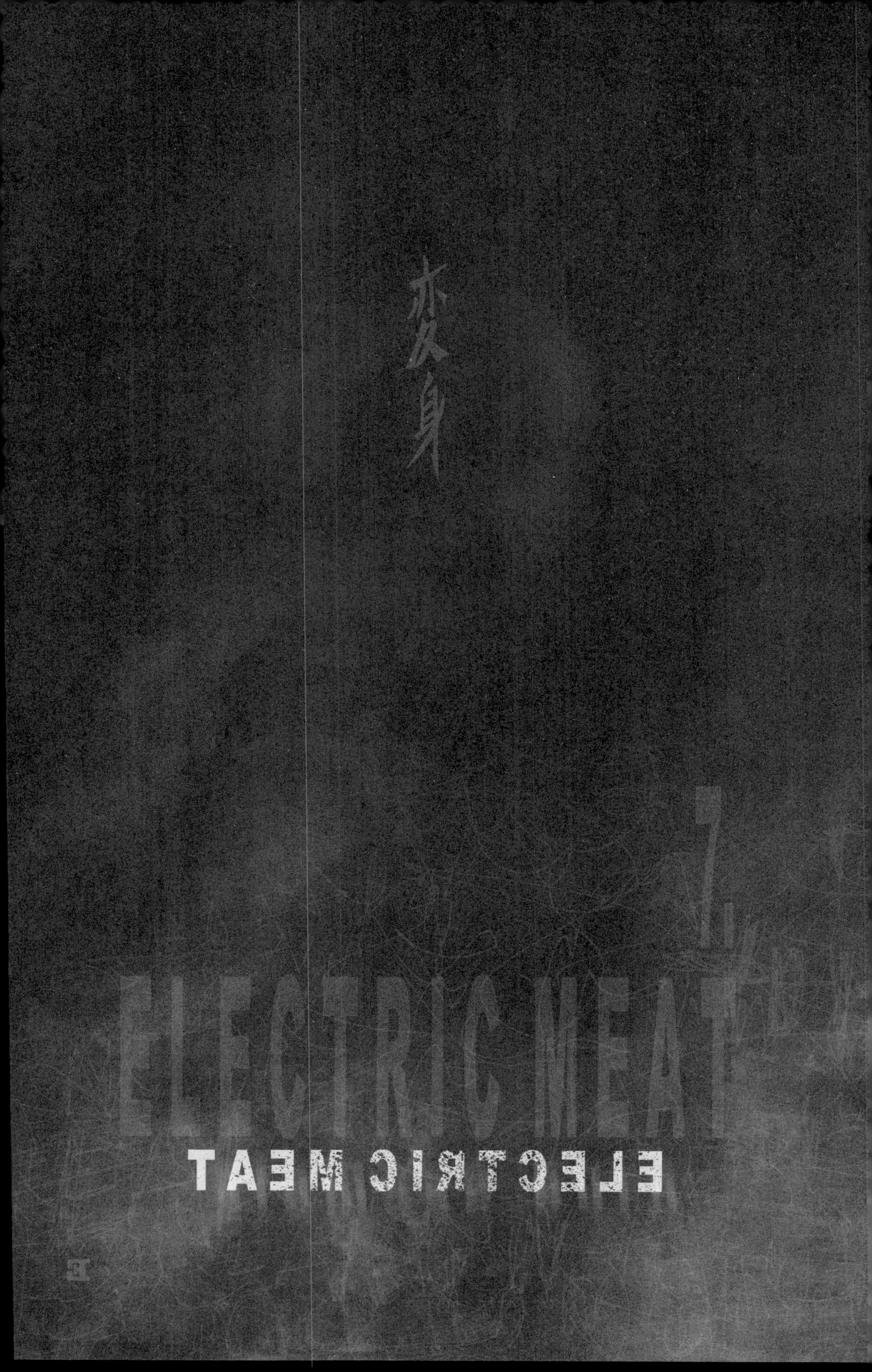
变身
7.
ELECTRIC MEAT
ELECTRIC MEAT

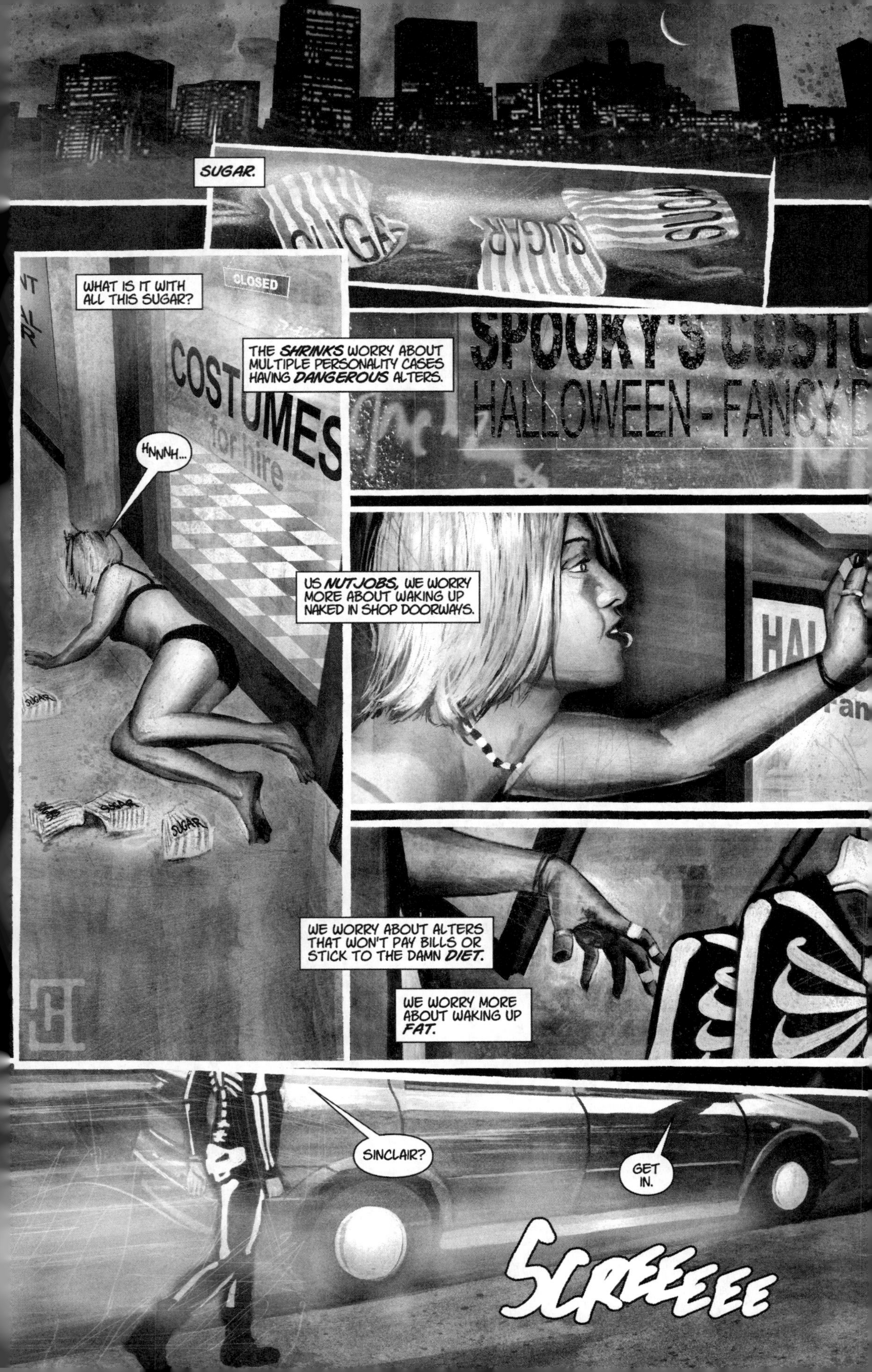

SUGAR.
SUGAR
SUGAR
SUGAR
WHAT IS IT WITH ALL THIS SUGAR?
CLOSED
COSTUMES for hire
THE SHRINKS WORRY ABOUT MULTIPLE PERSONALITY CASES HAVING DANGEROUS ALTERS.
SPOOKY'S COSTU
HALLOWEEN - FANCY D
HNNNH...
US NUTJOBS, WE WORRY MORE ABOUT WAKING UP NAKED IN SHOP DOORWAYS.
WE WORRY ABOUT ALTERS THAT WON'T PAY BILLS OR STICK TO THE DAMN DIET.
WE WORRY MORE ABOUT WAKING UP FAT.
SINCLAIR?
GET IN.
SCREEEEEE

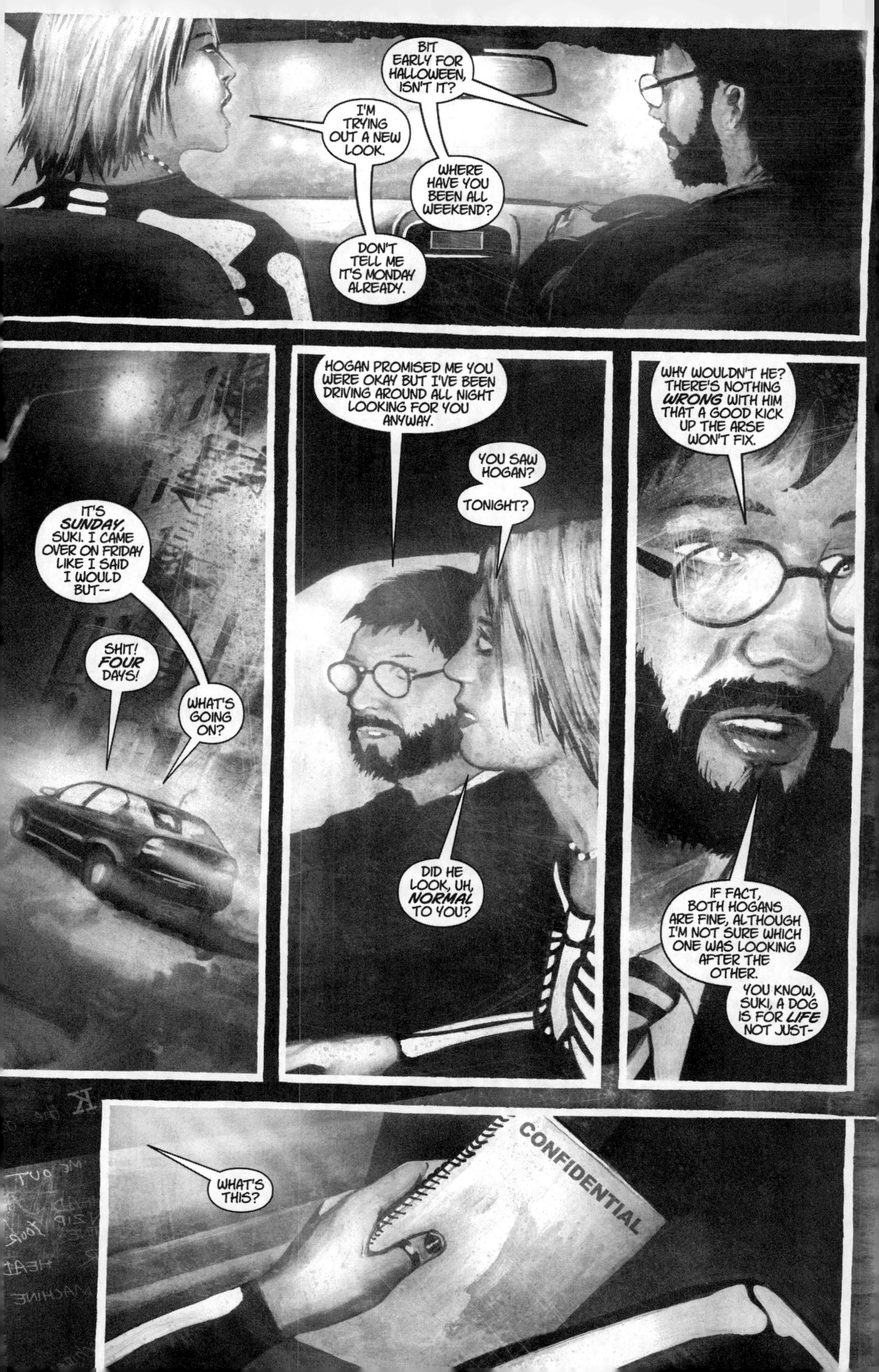
BIT EARLY FOR HALLOWEEN, ISN'T IT?
I'M TRYING OUT A NEW LOOK.
WHERE HAVE YOU BEEN ALL WEEKEND?
DON'T TELL ME IT'S MONDAY ALREADY.
IT'S *SUNDAY,* SUKI. I CAME OVER ON FRIDAY LIKE I SAID I WOULD BUT--
SHIT! *FOUR* DAYS!
WHAT'S GOING ON?
HOGAN PROMISED ME YOU WERE OKAY BUT I'VE BEEN DRIVING AROUND ALL NIGHT LOOKING FOR YOU ANYWAY.
YOU SAW HOGAN?
TONIGHT?
DID HE LOOK, UH, *NORMAL* TO YOU?
WHY WOULDN'T HE? THERE'S NOTHING *WRONG* WITH HIM THAT A GOOD KICK UP THE ARSE WON'T FIX.
IF FACT, BOTH HOGANS ARE FINE, ALTHOUGH I'M NOT SURE WHICH ONE WAS LOOKING AFTER THE OTHER.
YOU KNOW, SUKI, A DOG IS FOR *LIFE* NOT JUST-
WHAT'S THIS?
CONFIDENTIAL

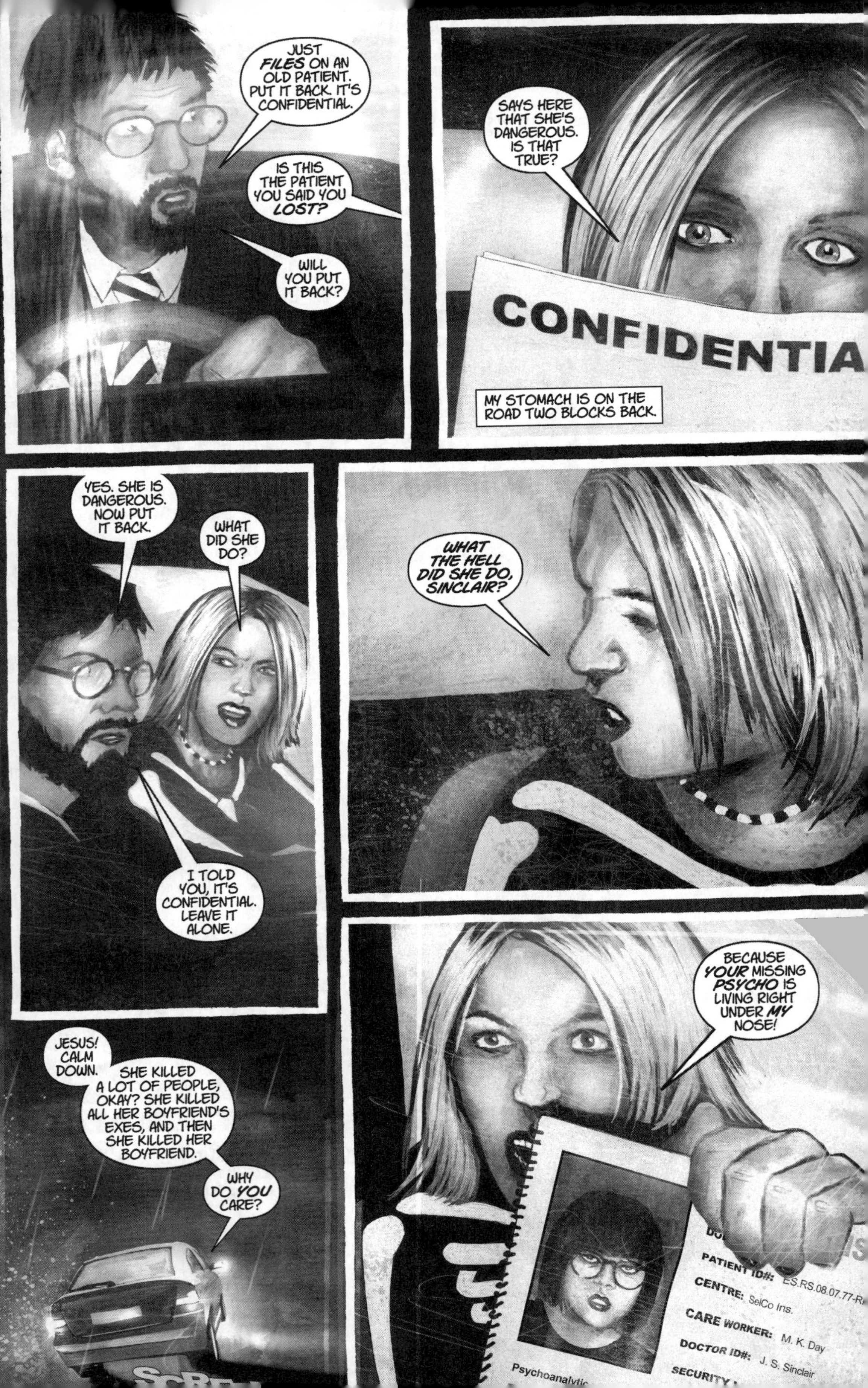
JUST FILES ON AN OLD PATIENT. PUT IT BACK. IT'S CONFIDENTIAL.
IS THIS THE PATIENT YOU SAID YOU LOST?
WILL YOU PUT IT BACK?
SAYS HERE THAT SHE'S DANGEROUS. IS THAT TRUE?
CONFIDENTIA
MY STOMACH IS ON THE ROAD TWO BLOCKS BACK.
YES. SHE IS DANGEROUS. NOW PUT IT BACK.
WHAT DID SHE DO?
I TOLD YOU, IT'S CONFIDENTIAL. LEAVE IT ALONE.
WHAT THE HELL DID SHE DO, SINCLAIR?
JESUS! CALM DOWN.
SHE KILLED A LOT OF PEOPLE, OKAY? SHE KILLED ALL HER BOYFRIEND'S EXES, AND THEN SHE KILLED HER BOYFRIEND.
WHY DO YOU CARE?
BECAUSE YOUR MISSING PSYCHO IS LIVING RIGHT UNDER MY NOSE!
PATIENT ID#: ES.RS.08.07.77-R
CENTRE: SelCo Ins.
CARE WORKER: M. K. Day
DOCTOR ID#: J. S. Sinclair
SECURITY
Psychoanalytic

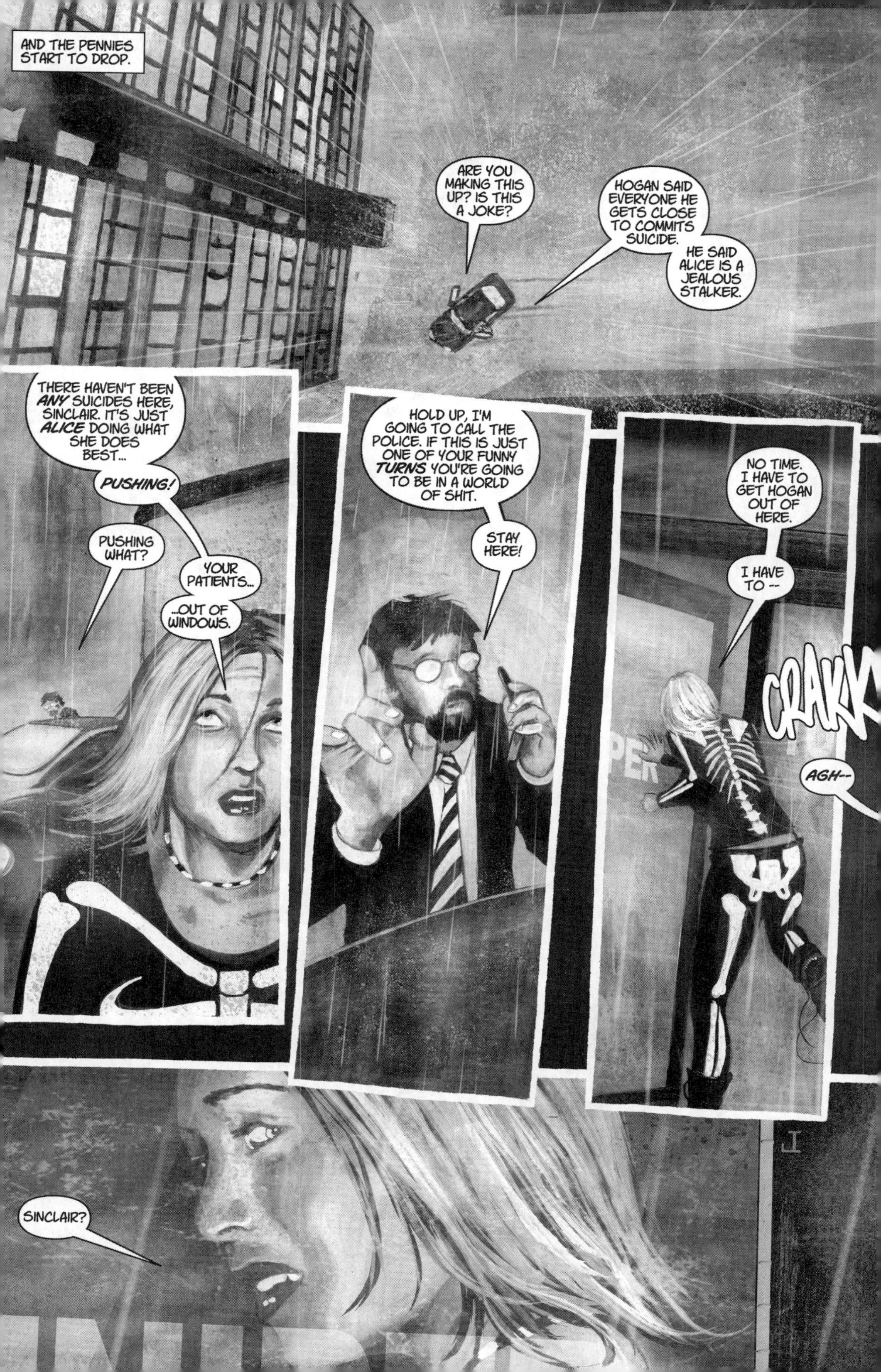
AND THE PENNIES START TO DROP.
ARE YOU MAKING THIS UP? IS THIS A JOKE?
HOGAN SAID EVERYONE HE GETS CLOSE TO COMMITS SUICIDE.
HE SAID ALICE IS A JEALOUS STALKER.
THERE HAVEN'T BEEN ANY SUICIDES HERE, SINCLAIR. IT'S JUST ALICE DOING WHAT SHE DOES BEST...
PUSHING!
PUSHING WHAT?
YOUR PATIENTS...
...OUT OF WINDOWS.
HOLD UP, I'M GOING TO CALL THE POLICE. IF THIS IS JUST ONE OF YOUR FUNNY TURNS YOU'RE GOING TO BE IN A WORLD OF SHIT.
STAY HERE!
NO TIME. I HAVE TO GET HOGAN OUT OF HERE.
I HAVE TO --
AGH--
SINCLAIR?

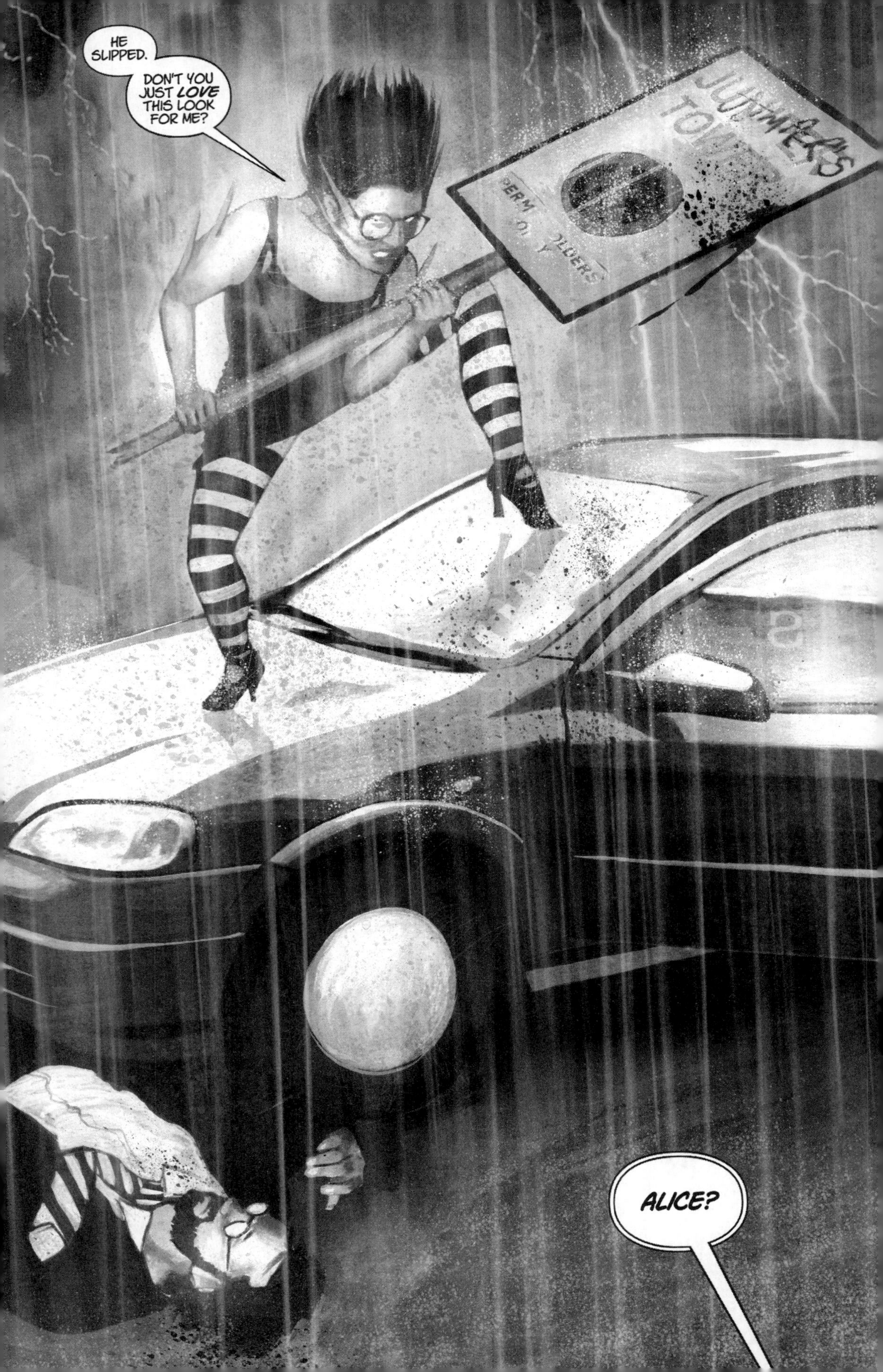
HE SLIPPED.
DON'T YOU JUST LOVE THIS LOOK FOR ME?
ALICE?

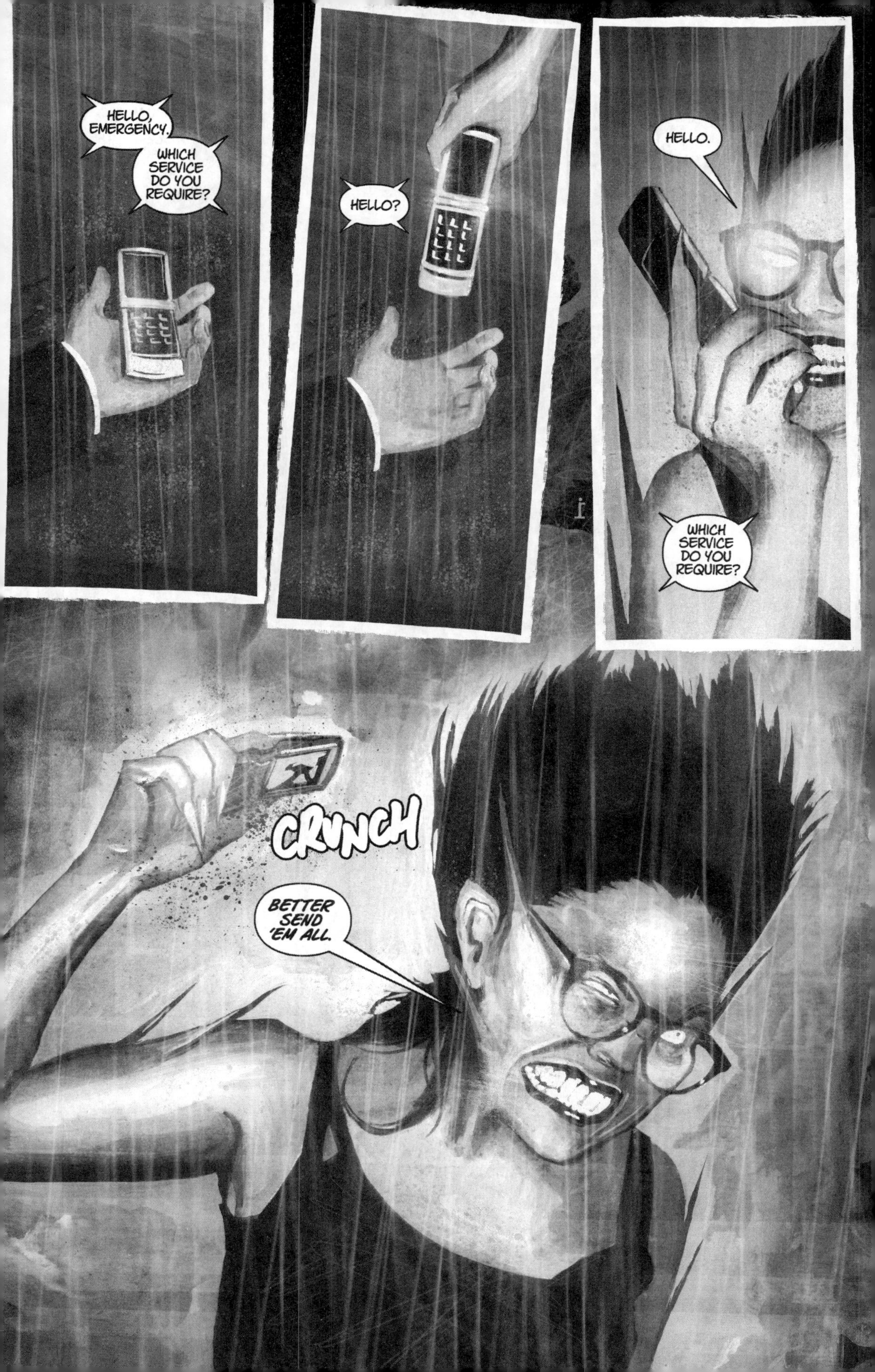
HELLO, EMERGENCY.
WHICH SERVICE DO YOU REQUIRE?
HELLO?
HELLO.
WHICH SERVICE DO YOU REQUIRE?
CRUNCH
BETTER SEND 'EM ALL.

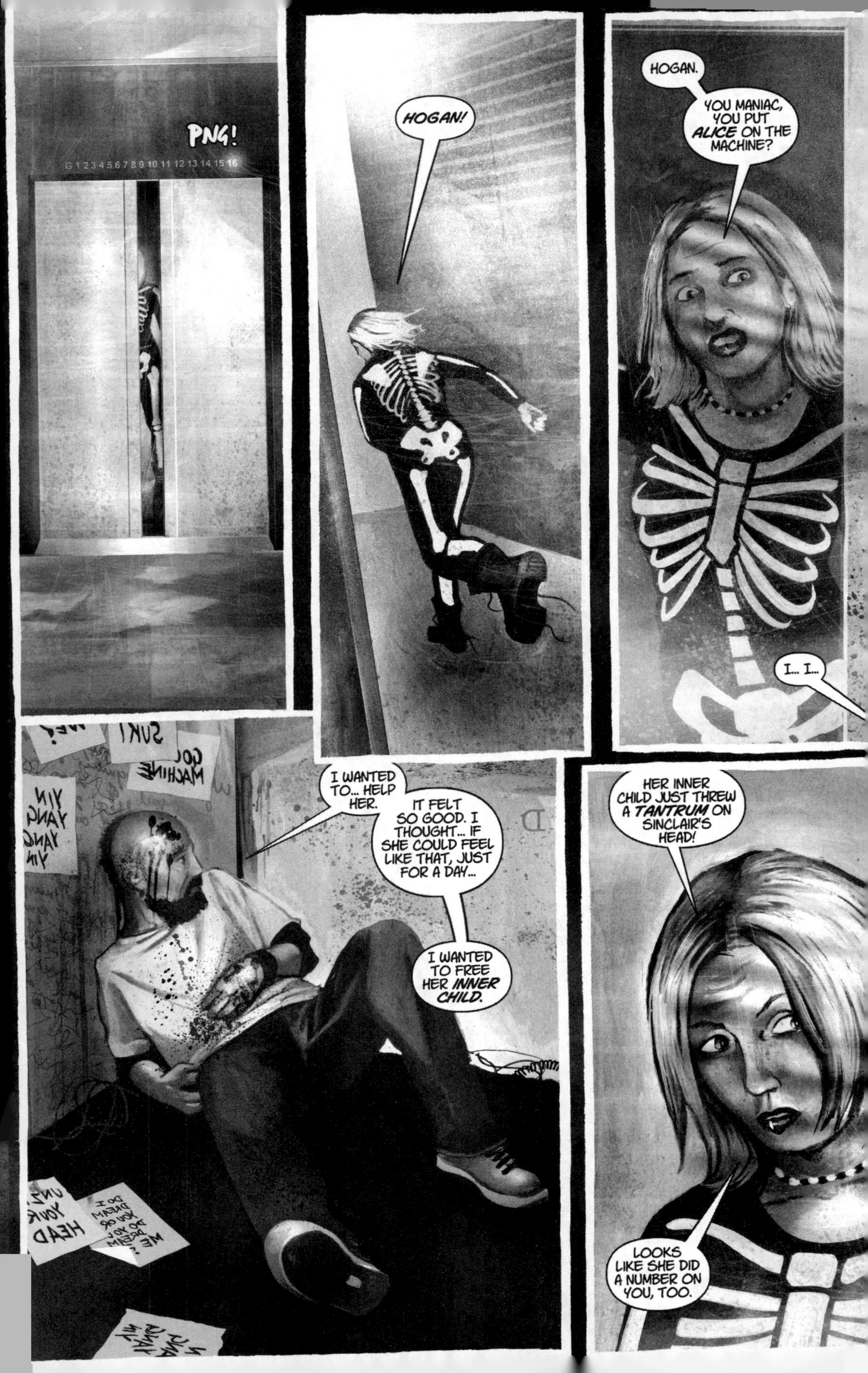
PNG!
G 1 2 3 4 5 6 7 8 9 10 11 12 13 14 15 16
HOGAN!
HOGAN.
YOU MANIAC, YOU PUT ALICE ON THE MACHINE?
I... I...
I WANTED TO... HELP HER.
IT FELT SO GOOD. I THOUGHT... IF SHE COULD FEEL LIKE THAT, JUST FOR A DAY...
I WANTED TO FREE HER INNER CHILD.
HER INNER CHILD JUST THREW A TANTRUM ON SINCLAIR'S HEAD!
LOOKS LIKE SHE DID A NUMBER ON YOU, TOO.

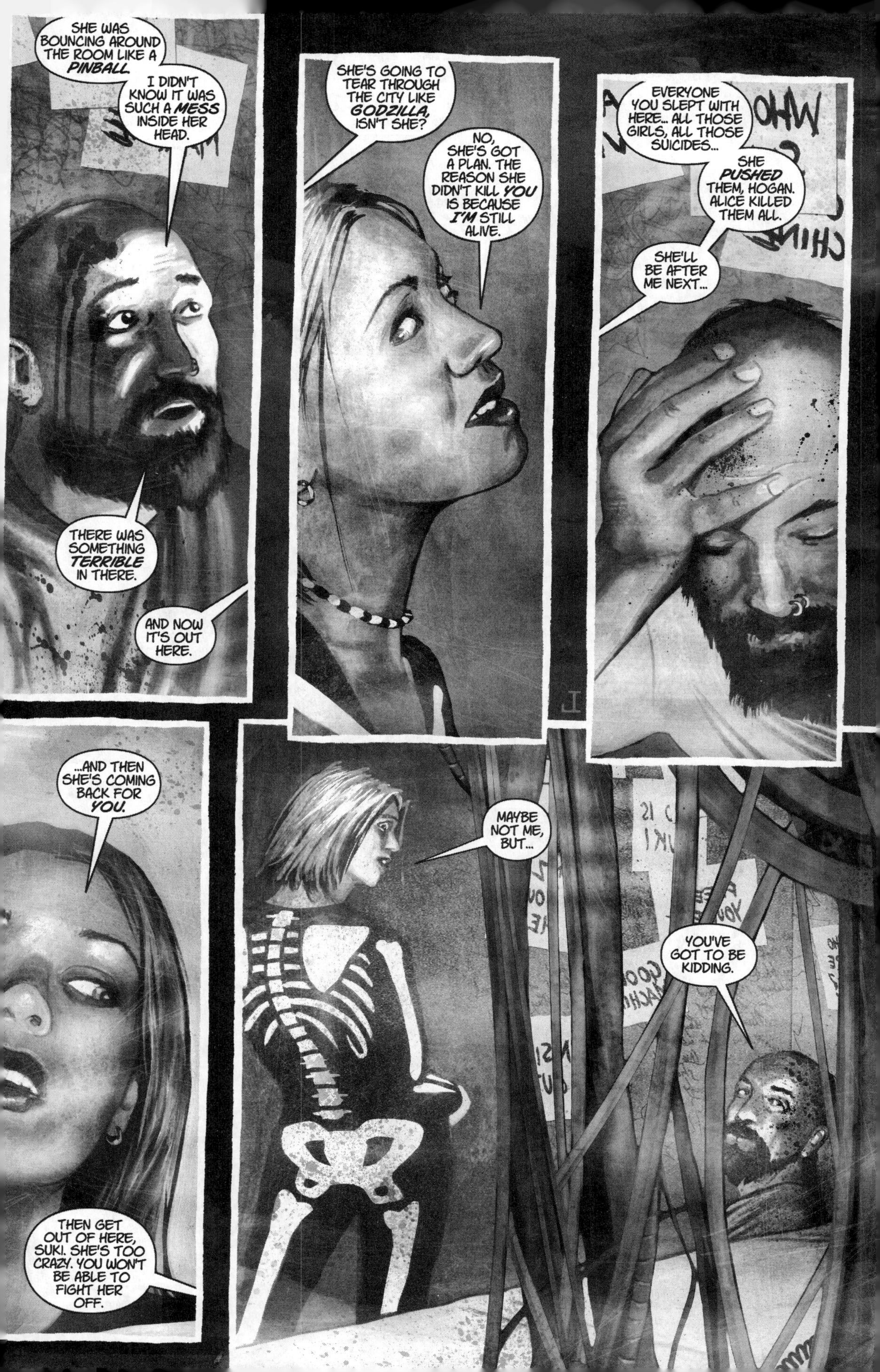
SHE WAS BOUNCING AROUND THE ROOM LIKE A PINBALL.
I DIDN'T KNOW IT WAS SUCH A MESS INSIDE HER HEAD.
THERE WAS SOMETHING TERRIBLE IN THERE.
AND NOW IT'S OUT HERE.
SHE'S GOING TO TEAR THROUGH THE CITY LIKE GODZILLA, ISN'T SHE?
NO, SHE'S GOT A PLAN. THE REASON SHE DIDN'T KILL YOU IS BECAUSE I'M STILL ALIVE.
EVERYONE YOU SLEPT WITH HERE... ALL THOSE GIRLS, ALL THOSE SUICIDES...
SHE PUSHED THEM, HOGAN. ALICE KILLED THEM ALL.
SHE'LL BE AFTER ME NEXT...
...AND THEN SHE'S COMING BACK FOR YOU.
THEN GET OUT OF HERE, SUKI. SHE'S TOO CRAZY. YOU WON'T BE ABLE TO FIGHT HER OFF.
MAYBE NOT ME, BUT...
YOU'VE GOT TO BE KIDDING.

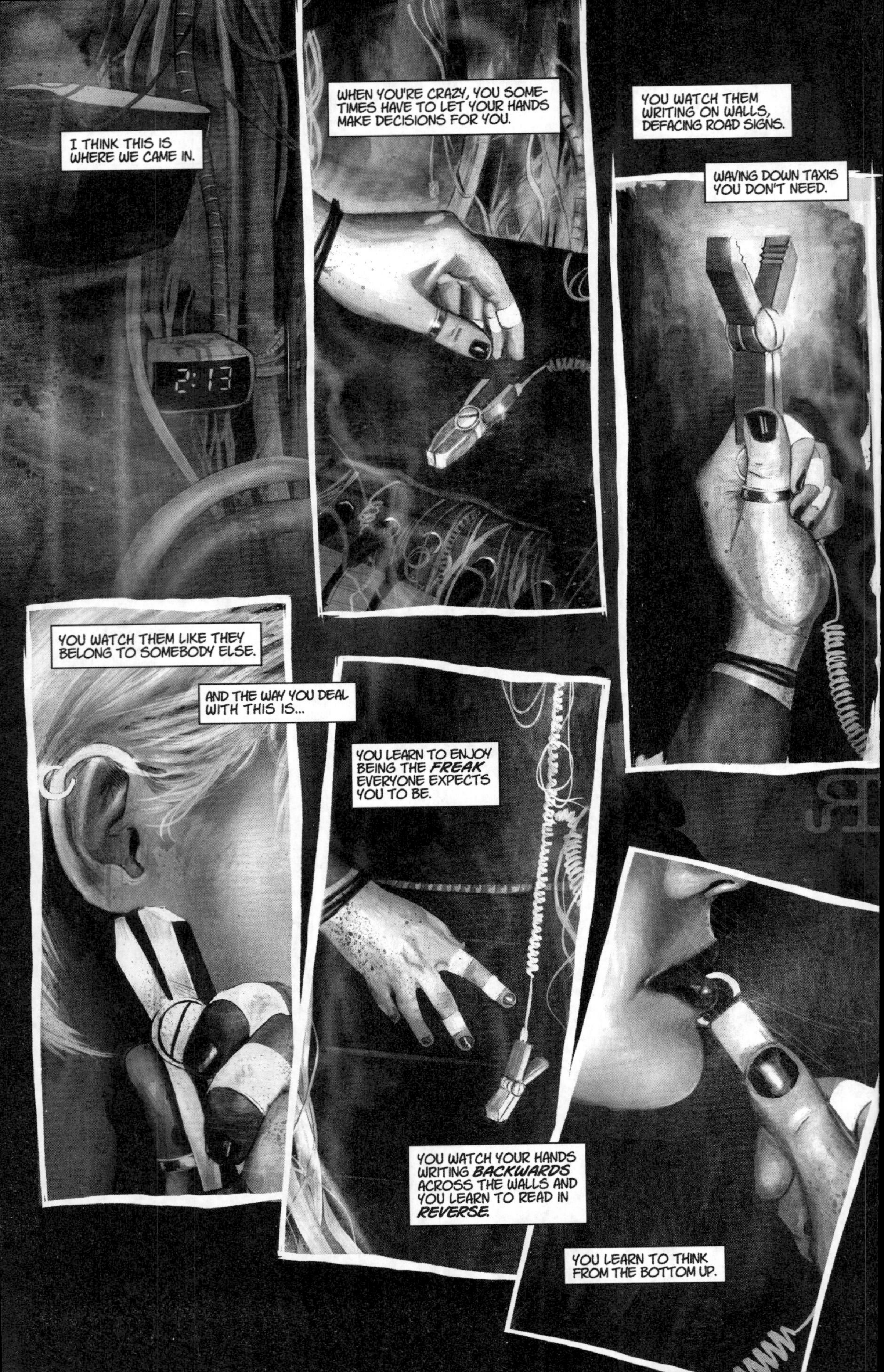
I THINK THIS IS WHERE WE CAME IN.
2:13
WHEN YOU'RE CRAZY, YOU SOMETIMES HAVE TO LET YOUR HANDS MAKE DECISIONS FOR YOU.
YOU WATCH THEM WRITING ON WALLS, DEFACING ROAD SIGNS.
WAVING DOWN TAXIS YOU DON'T NEED.
YOU WATCH THEM LIKE THEY BELONG TO SOMEBODY ELSE.
AND THE WAY YOU DEAL WITH THIS IS...
YOU LEARN TO ENJOY BEING THE *FREAK* EVERYONE EXPECTS YOU TO BE.
YOU WATCH YOUR HANDS WRITING *BACKWARDS* ACROSS THE WALLS AND YOU LEARN TO READ IN *REVERSE*.
YOU LEARN TO THINK FROM THE BOTTOM UP.

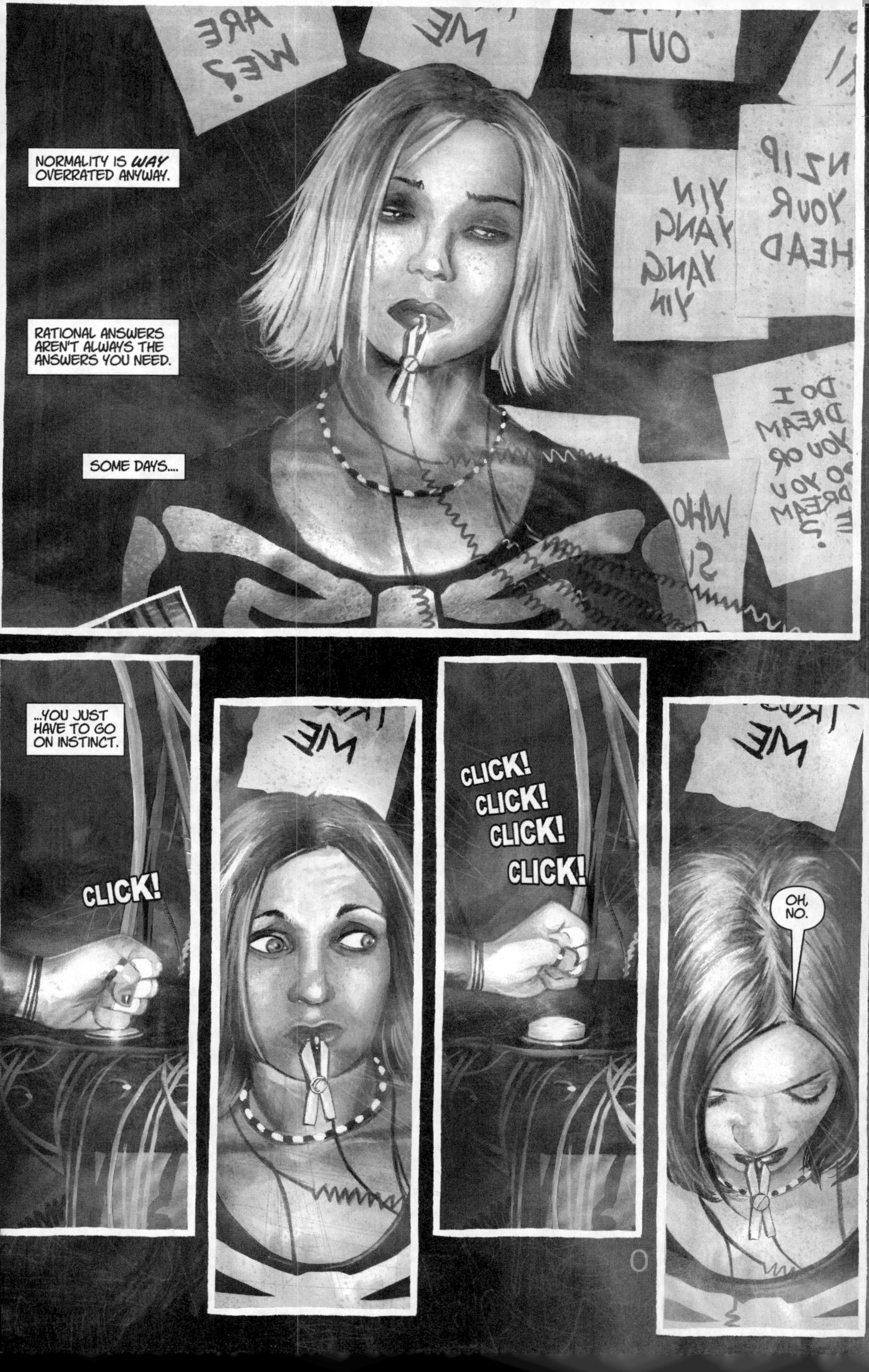
NORMALITY IS *WAY* OVERRATED ANYWAY.
RATIONAL ANSWERS AREN'T ALWAYS THE ANSWERS YOU NEED.
SOME DAYS....
...YOU JUST HAVE TO GO ON INSTINCT.
CLICK!
CLICK!
CLICK!
CLICK!
CLICK!
OH, NO.

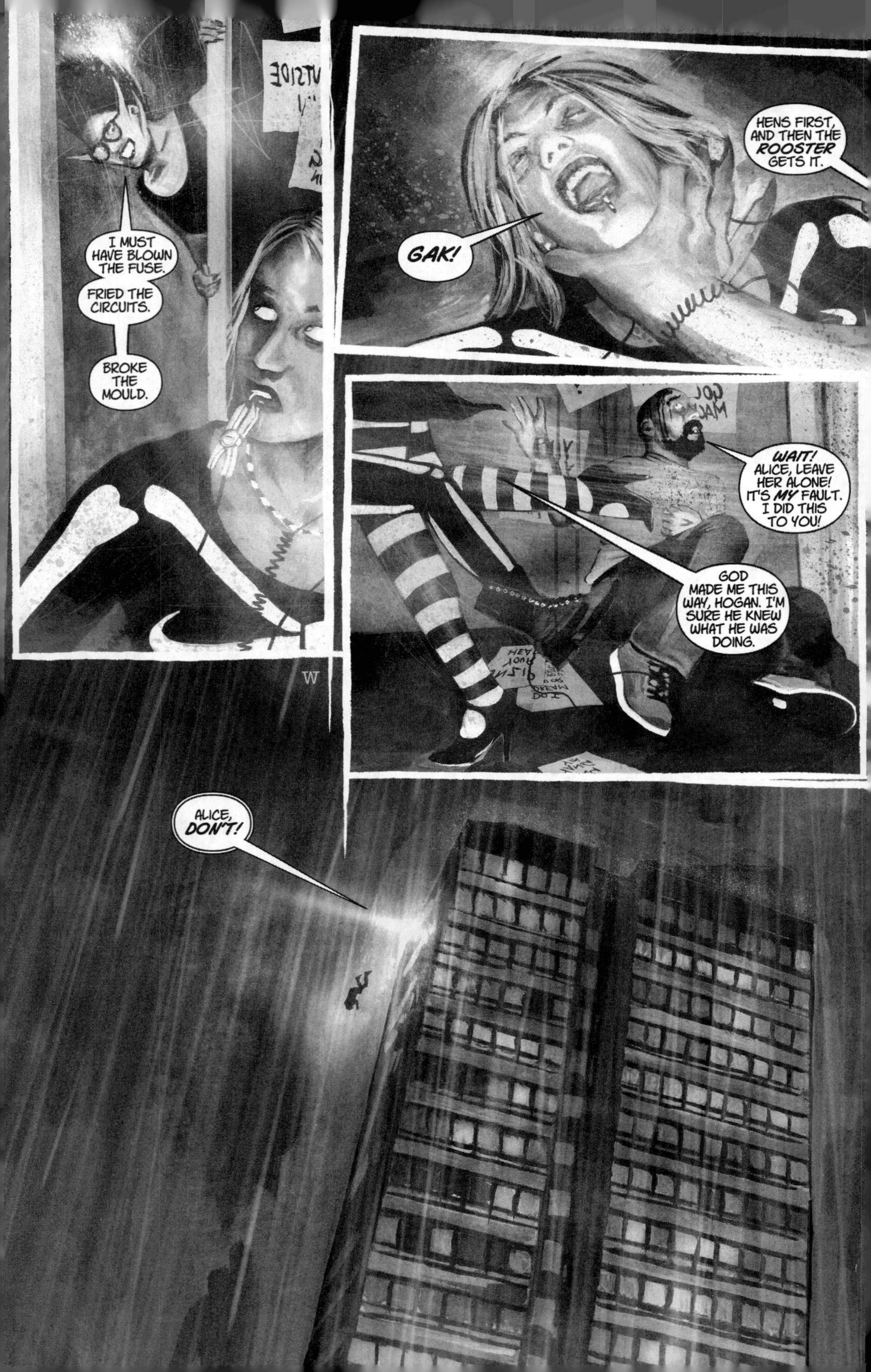
I MUST HAVE BLOWN THE FUSE.
FRIED THE CIRCUITS.
BROKE THE MOULD.
HENS FIRST, AND THEN THE ROOSTER GETS IT.
GAK!
WAIT! ALICE, LEAVE HER ALONE! IT'S MY FAULT. I DID THIS TO YOU!
GOD MADE ME THIS WAY, HOGAN. I'M SURE HE KNEW WHAT HE WAS DOING.
ALICE, DON'T!

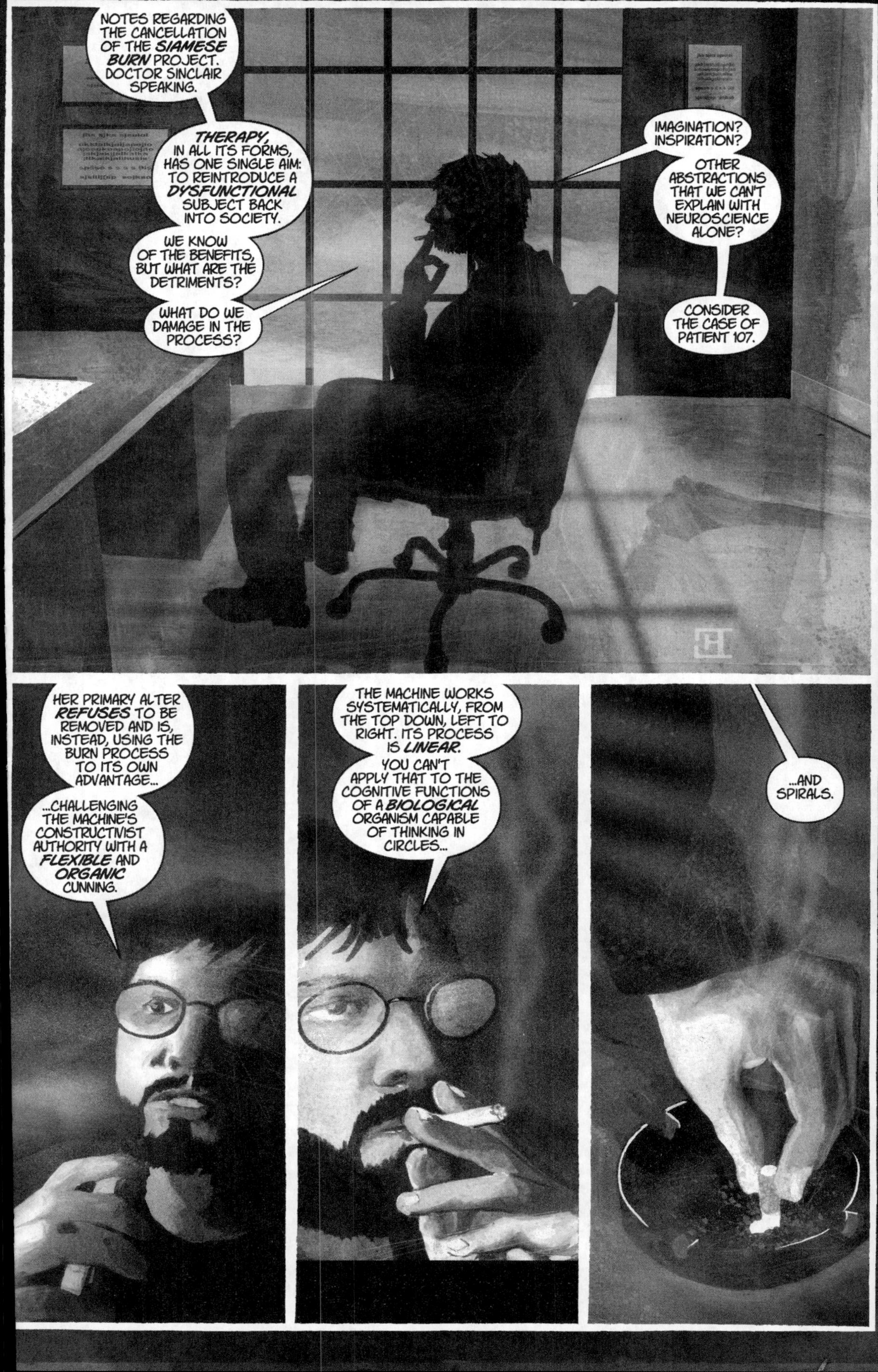
NOTES REGARDING THE CANCELLATION OF THE SIAMESE BURN PROJECT. DOCTOR SINCLAIR SPEAKING.
THERAPY, IN ALL ITS FORMS, HAS ONE SINGLE AIM: TO REINTRODUCE A DYSFUNCTIONAL SUBJECT BACK INTO SOCIETY.
WE KNOW OF THE BENEFITS, BUT WHAT ARE THE DETRIMENTS?
WHAT DO WE DAMAGE IN THE PROCESS?
IMAGINATION? INSPIRATION?
OTHER ABSTRACTIONS THAT WE CAN'T EXPLAIN WITH NEUROSCIENCE ALONE?
CONSIDER THE CASE OF PATIENT 107.
HER PRIMARY ALTER REFUSES TO BE REMOVED AND IS, INSTEAD, USING THE BURN PROCESS TO ITS OWN ADVANTAGE...
...CHALLENGING THE MACHINE'S CONSTRUCTIVIST AUTHORITY WITH A FLEXIBLE AND ORGANIC CUNNING.
THE MACHINE WORKS SYSTEMATICALLY, FROM THE TOP DOWN, LEFT TO RIGHT. ITS PROCESS IS LINEAR.
YOU CAN'T APPLY THAT TO THE COGNITIVE FUNCTIONS OF A BIOLOGICAL ORGANISM CAPABLE OF THINKING IN CIRCLES...
...AND SPIRALS.

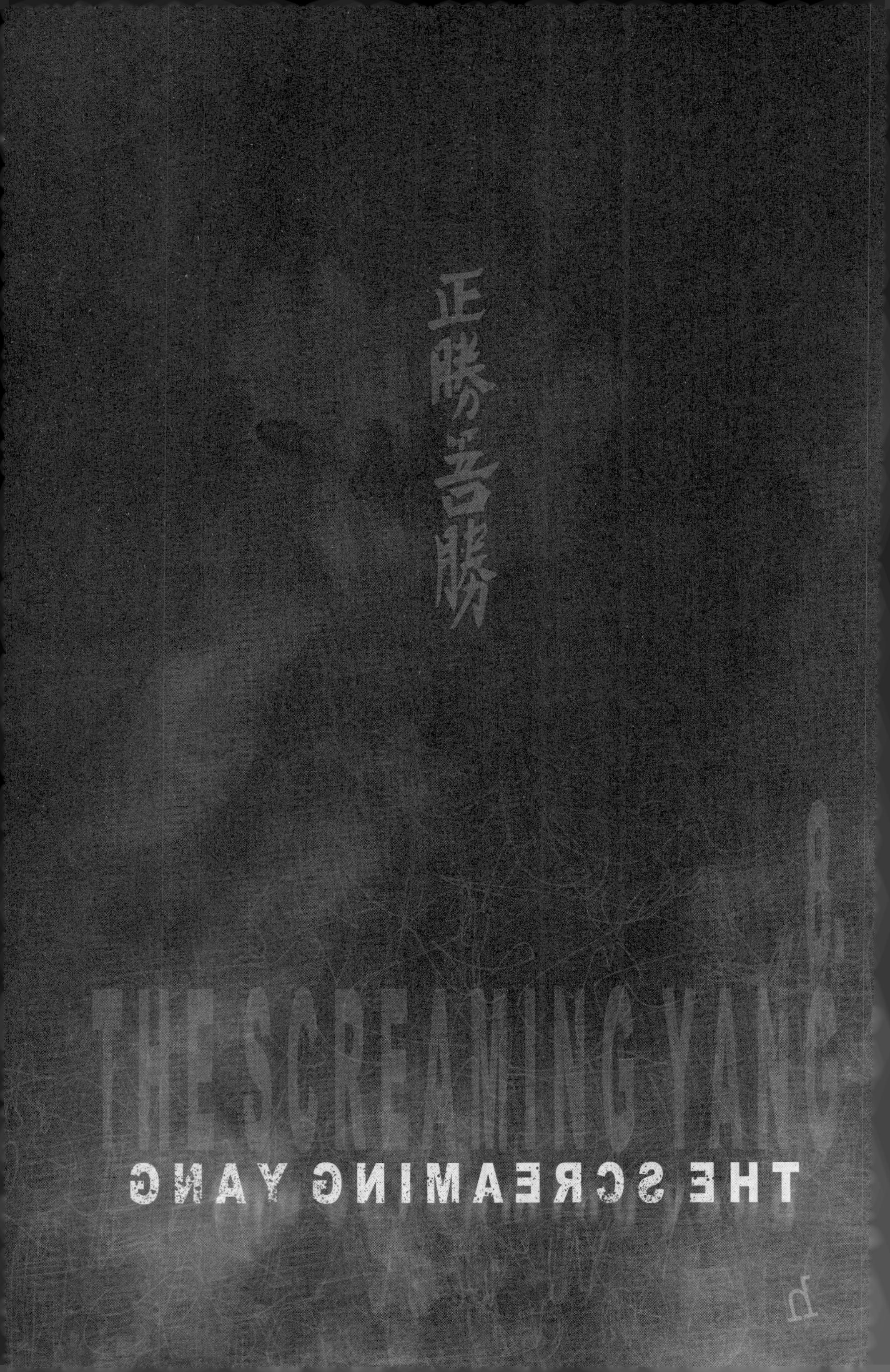
正勝吾勝
THE SCREAMING YANG 8
THE SCREAMING YANG

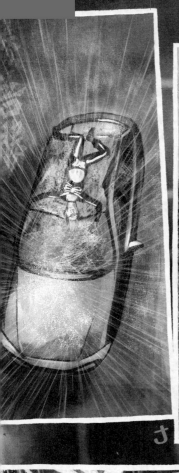

THEY SAY MADNESS IS CULTURALLY RELATIVE...

...BUT I CAN'T IMAGINE *THIS* WOULD GO DOWN WELL ANYWHERE.

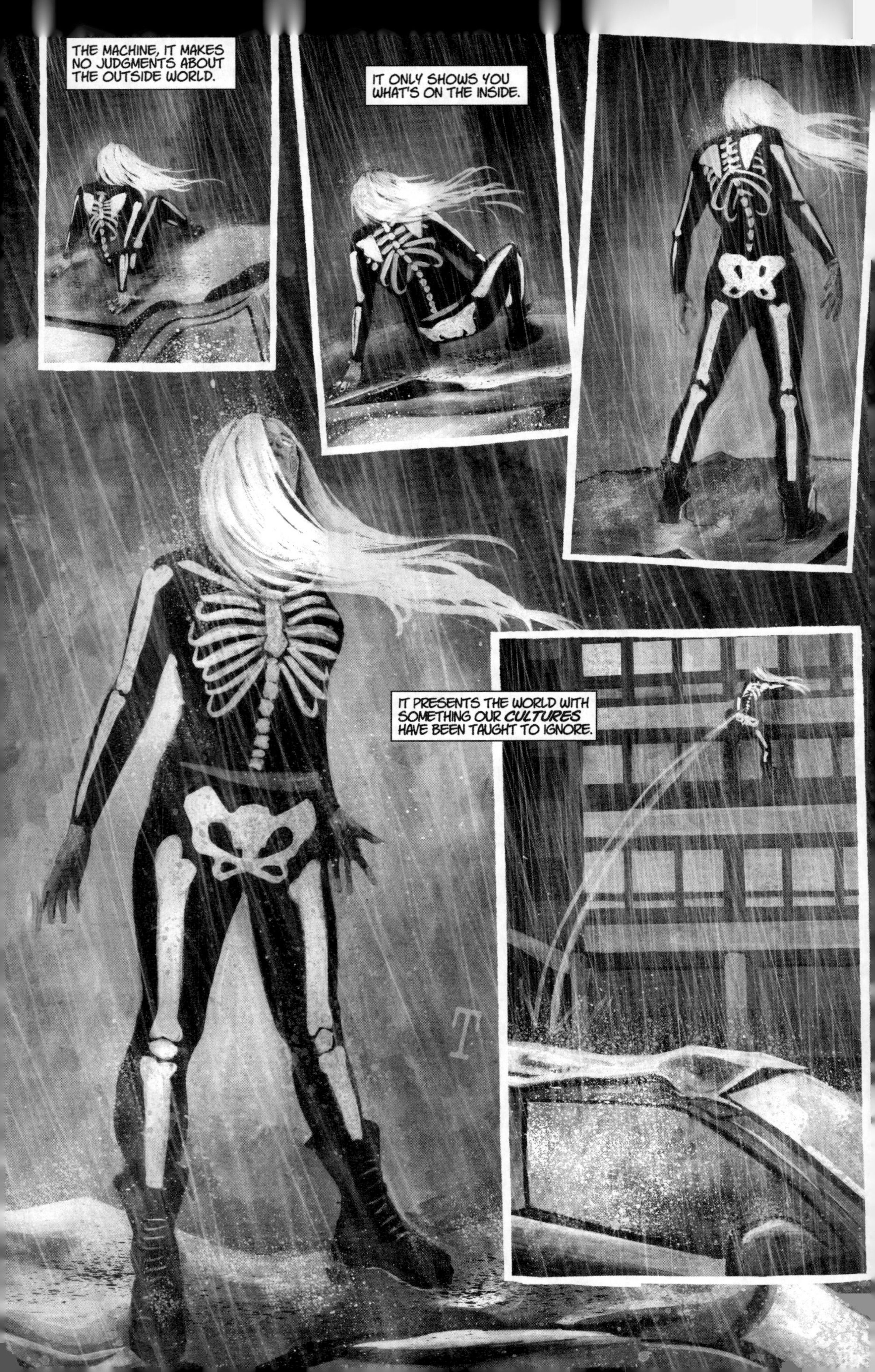
THE MACHINE, IT MAKES NO JUDGMENTS ABOUT THE OUTSIDE WORLD.
IT ONLY SHOWS YOU WHAT'S ON THE INSIDE.
IT PRESENTS THE WORLD WITH SOMETHING OUR *CULTURES* HAVE BEEN TAUGHT TO IGNORE.

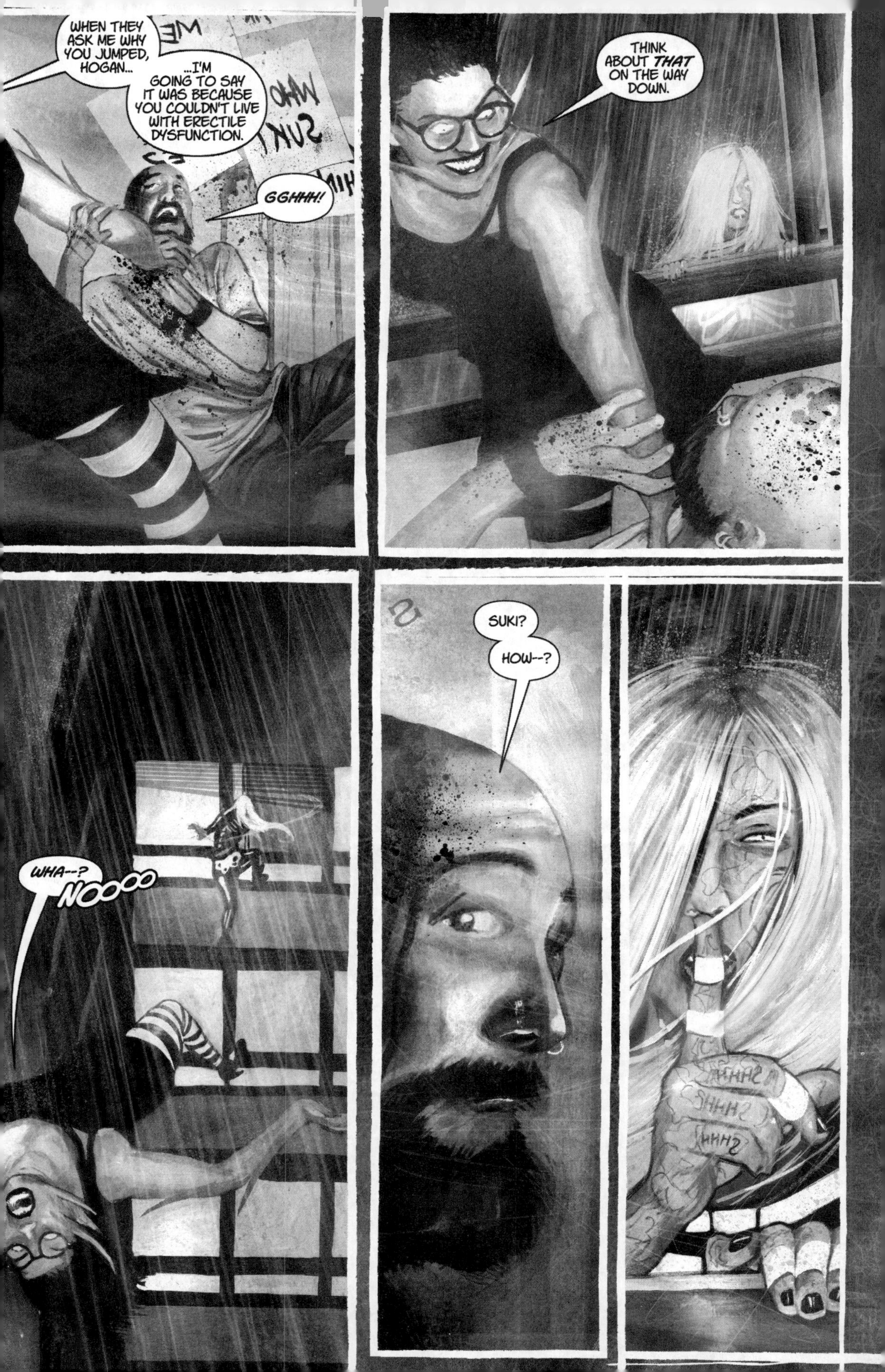

WHEN THEY ASK ME WHY YOU JUMPED, HOGAN...
...I'M GOING TO SAY IT WAS BECAUSE YOU COULDN'T LIVE WITH ERECTILE DYSFUNCTION.
GGHHH!
THINK ABOUT *THAT* ON THE WAY DOWN.
WHA--? NOOOO
SUKI?
HOW--?

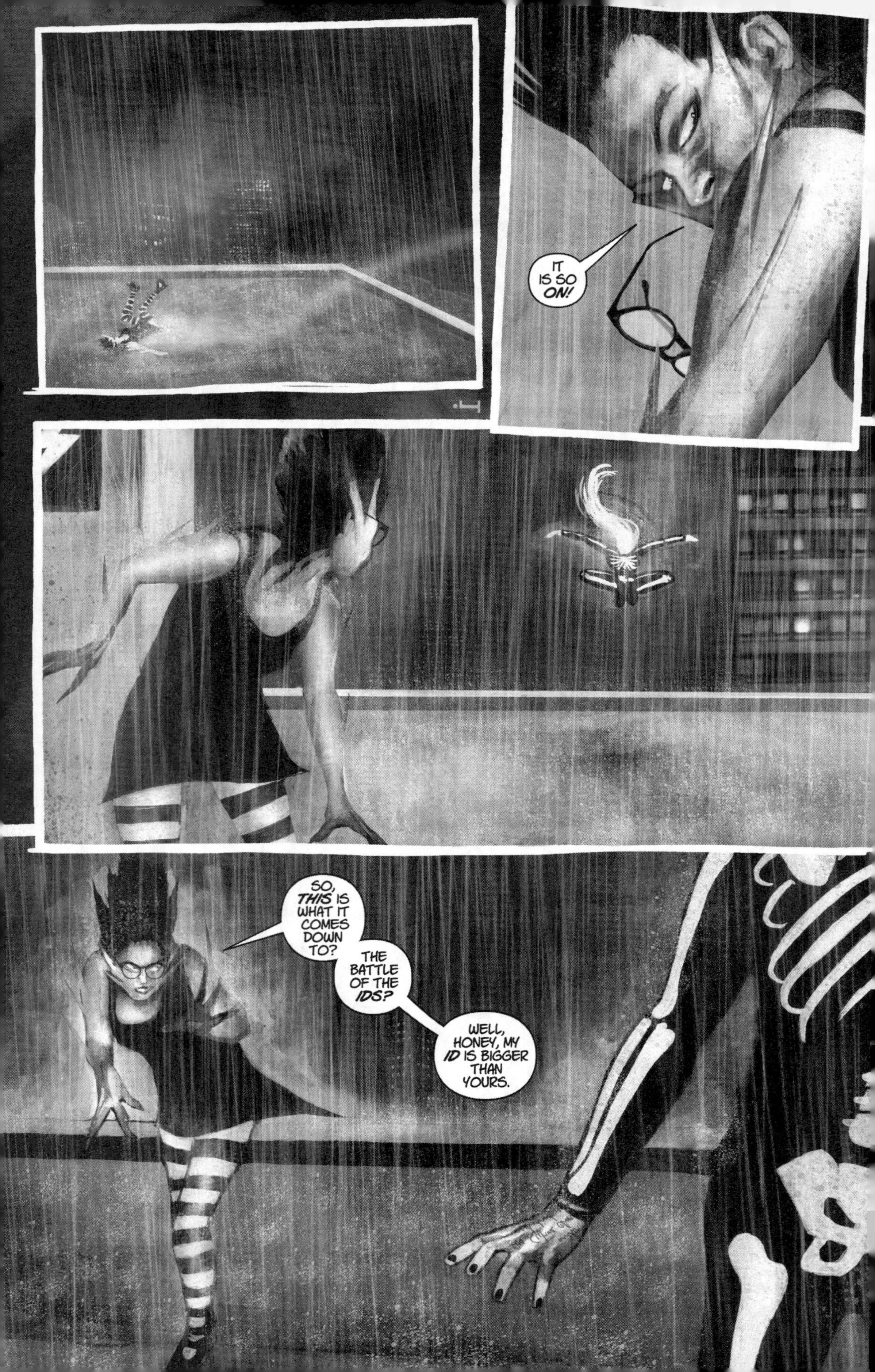
IT IS SO ON!
SO, THIS IS WHAT IT COMES DOWN TO?
THE BATTLE OF THE IDS?
WELL, HONEY, MY ID IS BIGGER THAN YOURS.

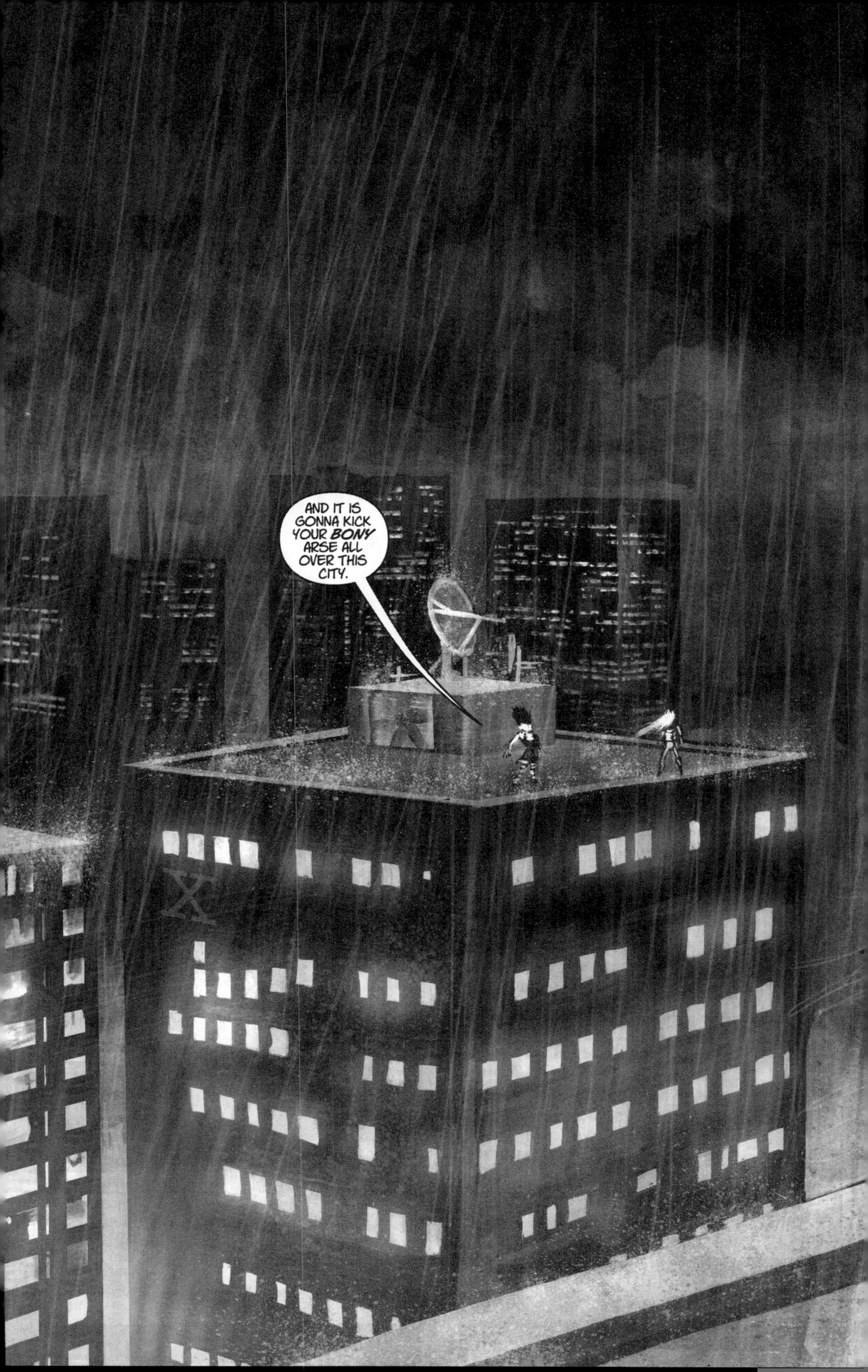
AND IT IS GONNA KICK YOUR BONY ARSE ALL OVER THIS CITY.

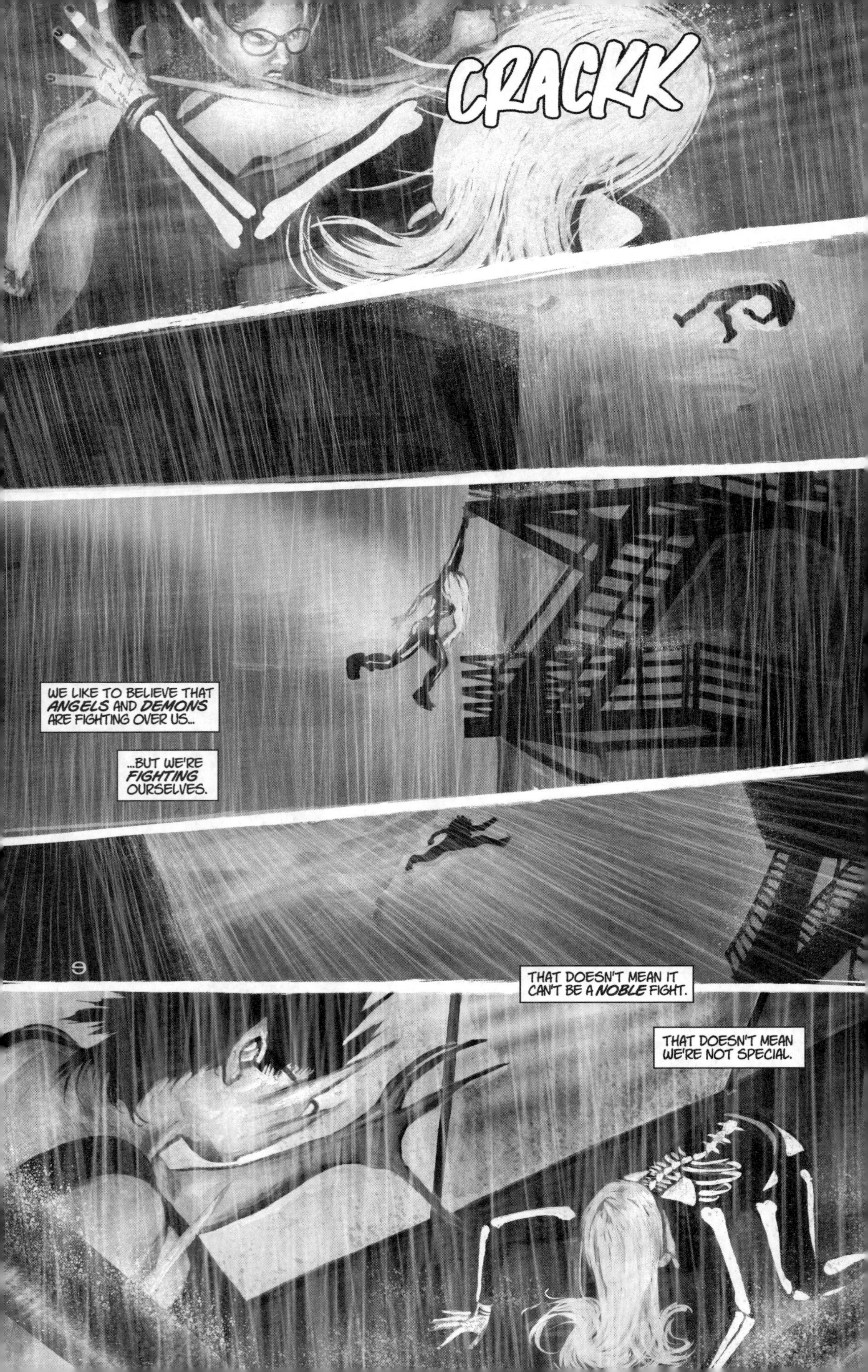
CRACKK
WE LIKE TO BELIEVE THAT ANGELS AND DEMONS ARE FIGHTING OVER US...
...BUT WE'RE FIGHTING OURSELVES.
THAT DOESN'T MEAN IT CAN'T BE A NOBLE FIGHT.
THAT DOESN'T MEAN WE'RE NOT SPECIAL.

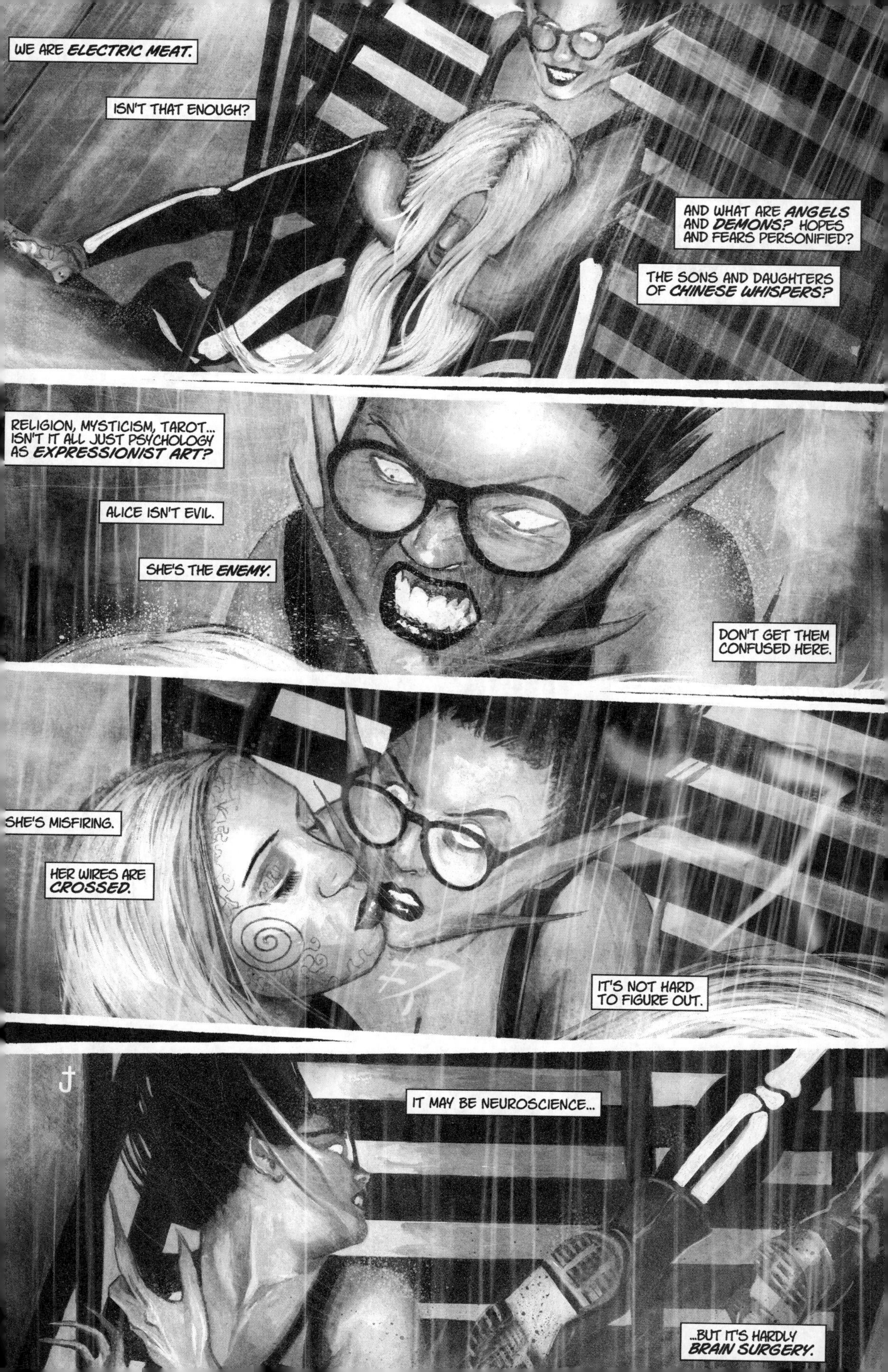
WE ARE ELECTRIC MEAT.
ISN'T THAT ENOUGH?
AND WHAT ARE ANGELS AND DEMONS? HOPES AND FEARS PERSONIFIED?
THE SONS AND DAUGHTERS OF CHINESE WHISPERS?
RELIGION, MYSTICISM, TAROT... ISN'T IT ALL JUST PSYCHOLOGY AS EXPRESSIONIST ART?
ALICE ISN'T EVIL.
SHE'S THE ENEMY.
DON'T GET THEM CONFUSED HERE.
SHE'S MISFIRING.
HER WIRES ARE CROSSED.
IT'S NOT HARD TO FIGURE OUT.
IT MAY BE NEUROSCIENCE...
...BUT IT'S HARDLY BRAIN SURGERY.

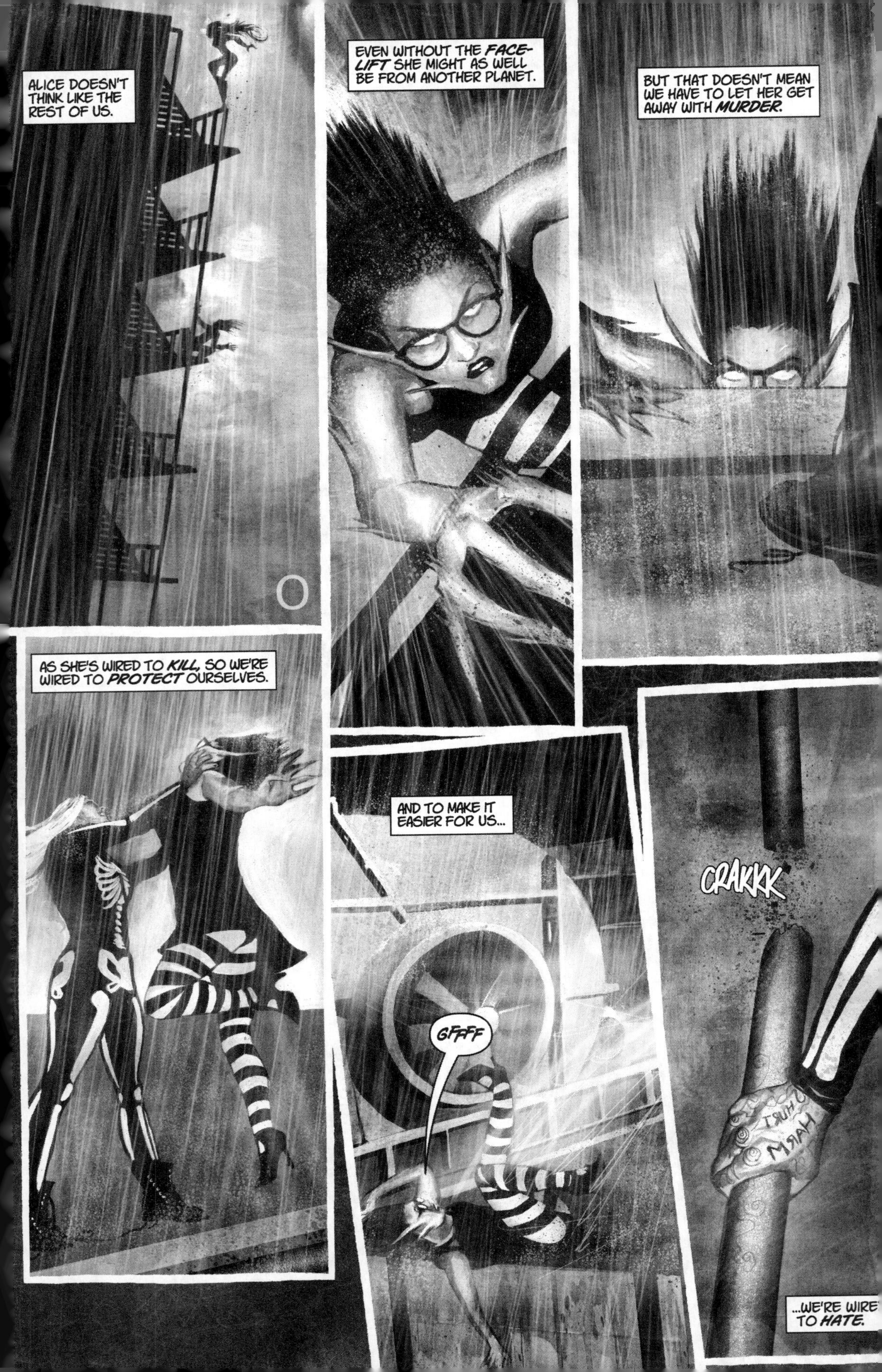

ALICE DOESN'T THINK LIKE THE REST OF US.
EVEN WITHOUT THE *FACE-LIFT* SHE MIGHT AS WELL BE FROM ANOTHER PLANET.
BUT THAT DOESN'T MEAN WE HAVE TO LET HER GET AWAY WITH *MURDER*.
AS SHE'S WIRED TO *KILL*, SO WE'RE WIRED TO *PROTECT* OURSELVES.
AND TO MAKE IT EASIER FOR US...
GFFFF
CRAKKK
...WE'RE WIRE TO *HATE*.

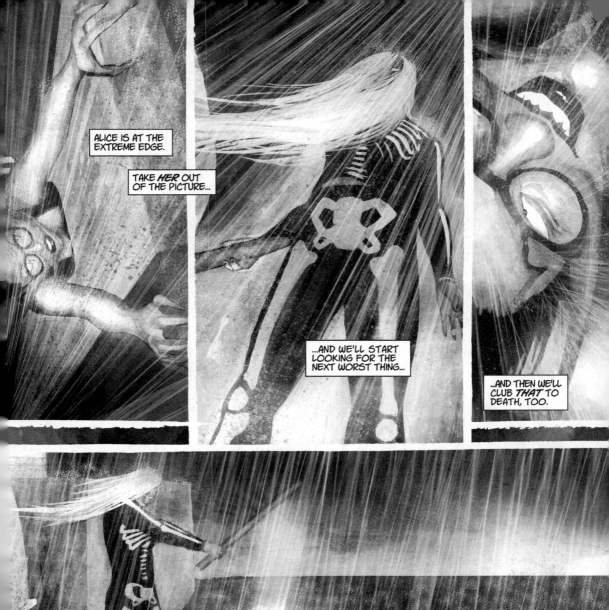

ALICE IS AT THE EXTREME EDGE.

TAKE *HER* OUT OF THE PICTURE...

...AND WE'LL START LOOKING FOR THE NEXT WORST THING...

...AND THEN WE'LL CLUB *THAT* TO DEATH, TOO.

CHNNNG

KTSSCH

THE WORD *EVIL* IS A SHORTCUT LABEL FOR ALICE.

OUR BELIEFS, HER BELIEFS...

...THEY'RE THE *SUGAR* THAT MAKES THE TRUTH EASIER TO SWALLOW.

THEY'RE ALSO THE FUEL ON THE *FIRE*.

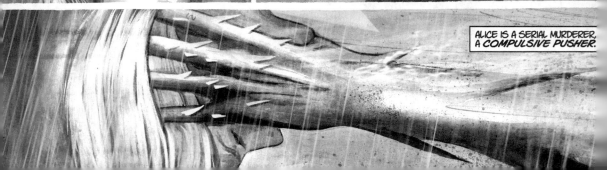

ALICE IS A SERIAL MURDERER, A *COMPULSIVE PUSHER*.

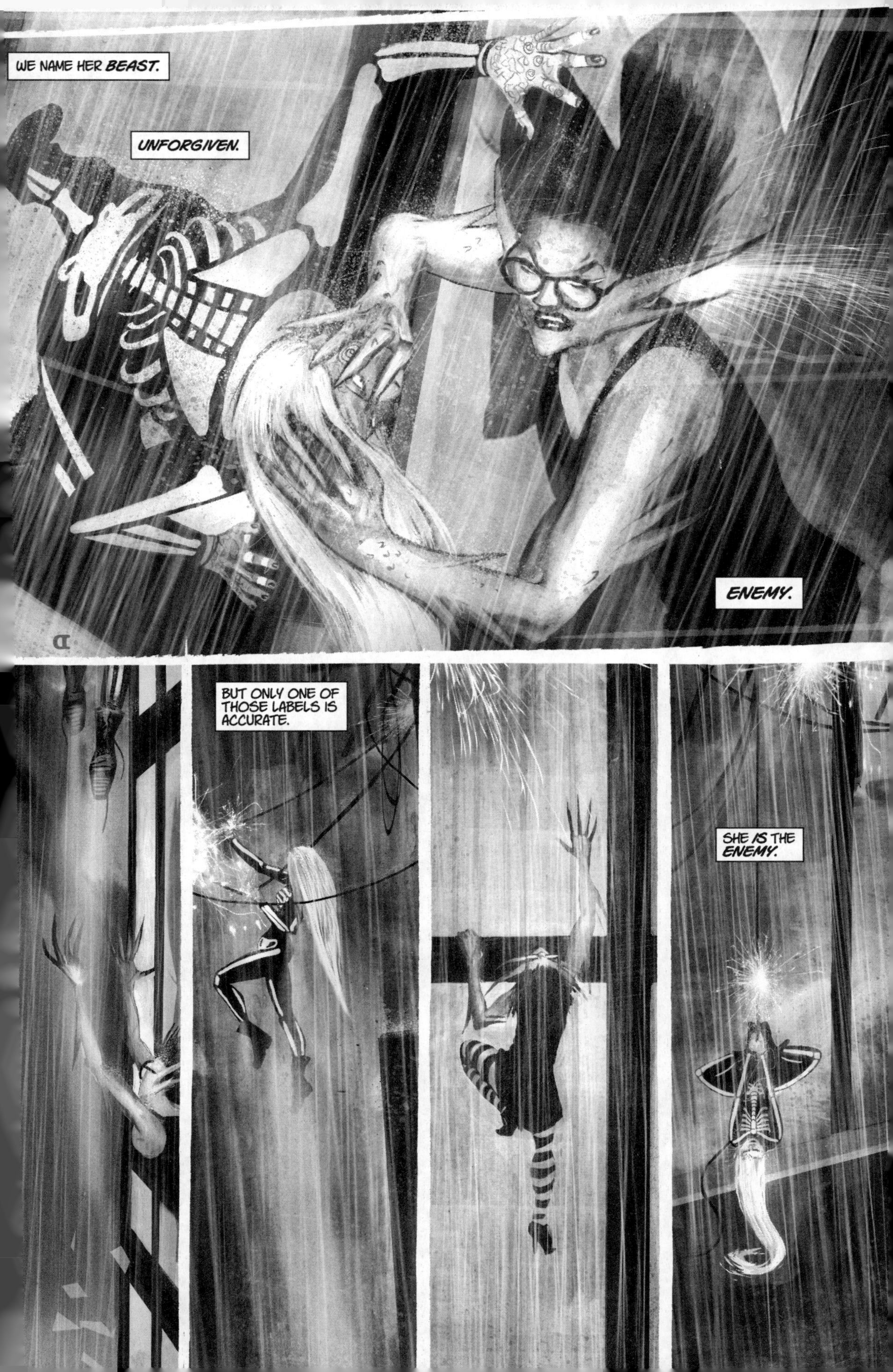
WE NAME HER BEAST.
UNFORGIVEN.
ENEMY.
BUT ONLY ONE OF THOSE LABELS IS ACCURATE.
SHE IS THE ENEMY.

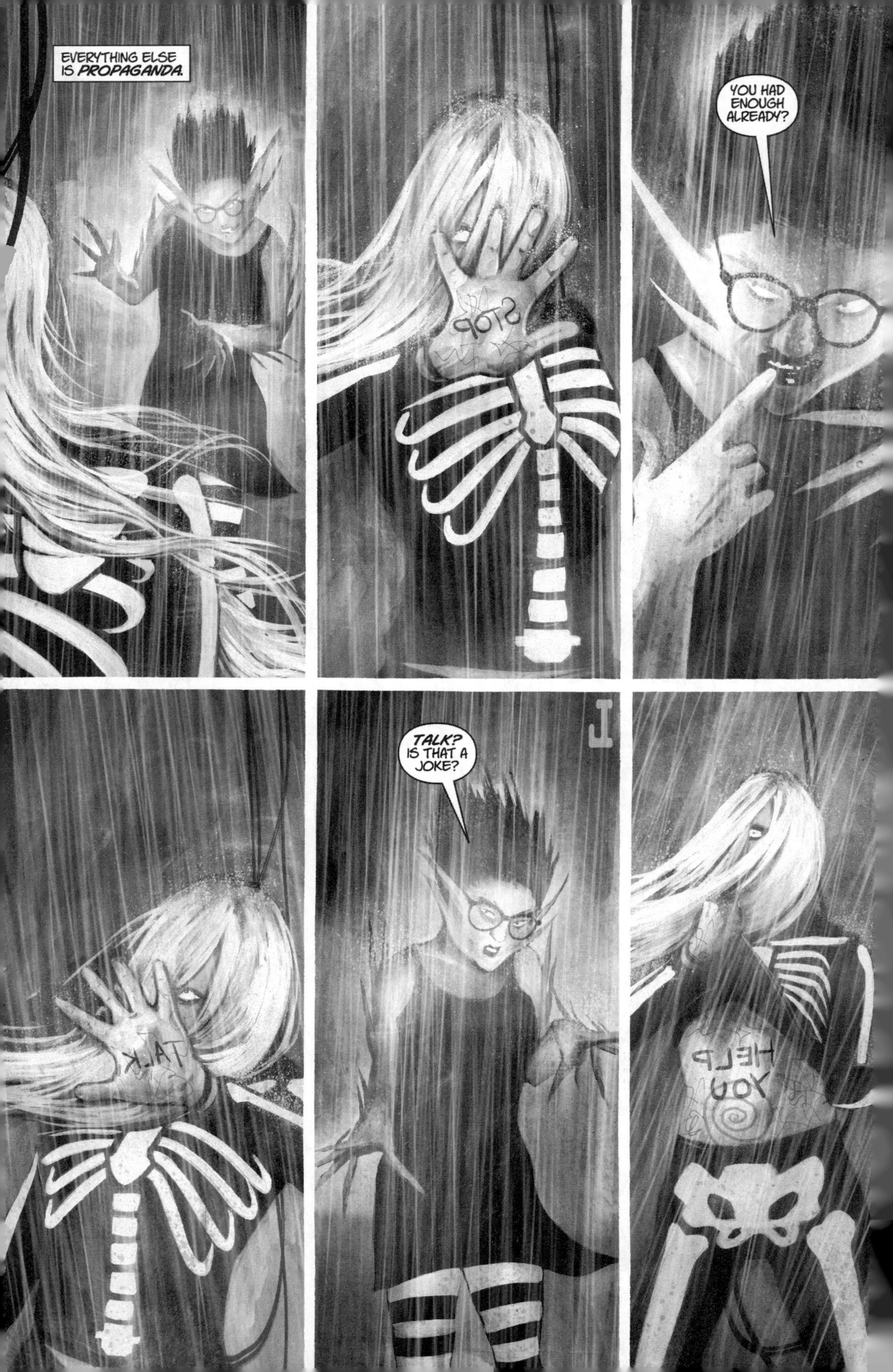
EVERYTHING ELSE IS *PROPAGANDA*.
STOP
YOU HAD ENOUGH ALREADY?
TALK
TALK? IS THAT A JOKE?
HELP YOU

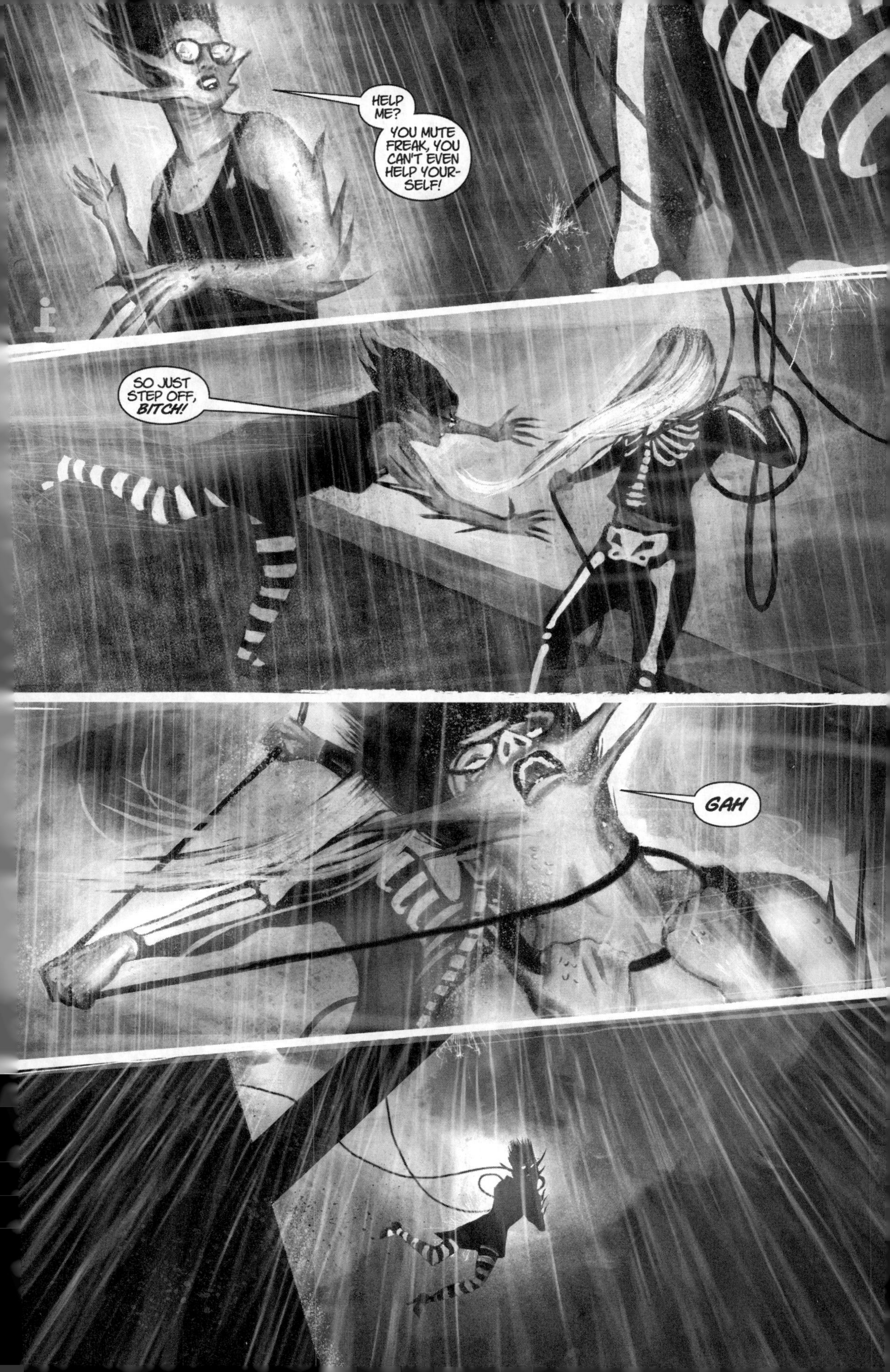
HELP ME?
YOU MUTE FREAK, YOU CAN'T EVEN HELP YOUR-SELF!
SO JUST STEP OFF, *BITCH!*
GAH

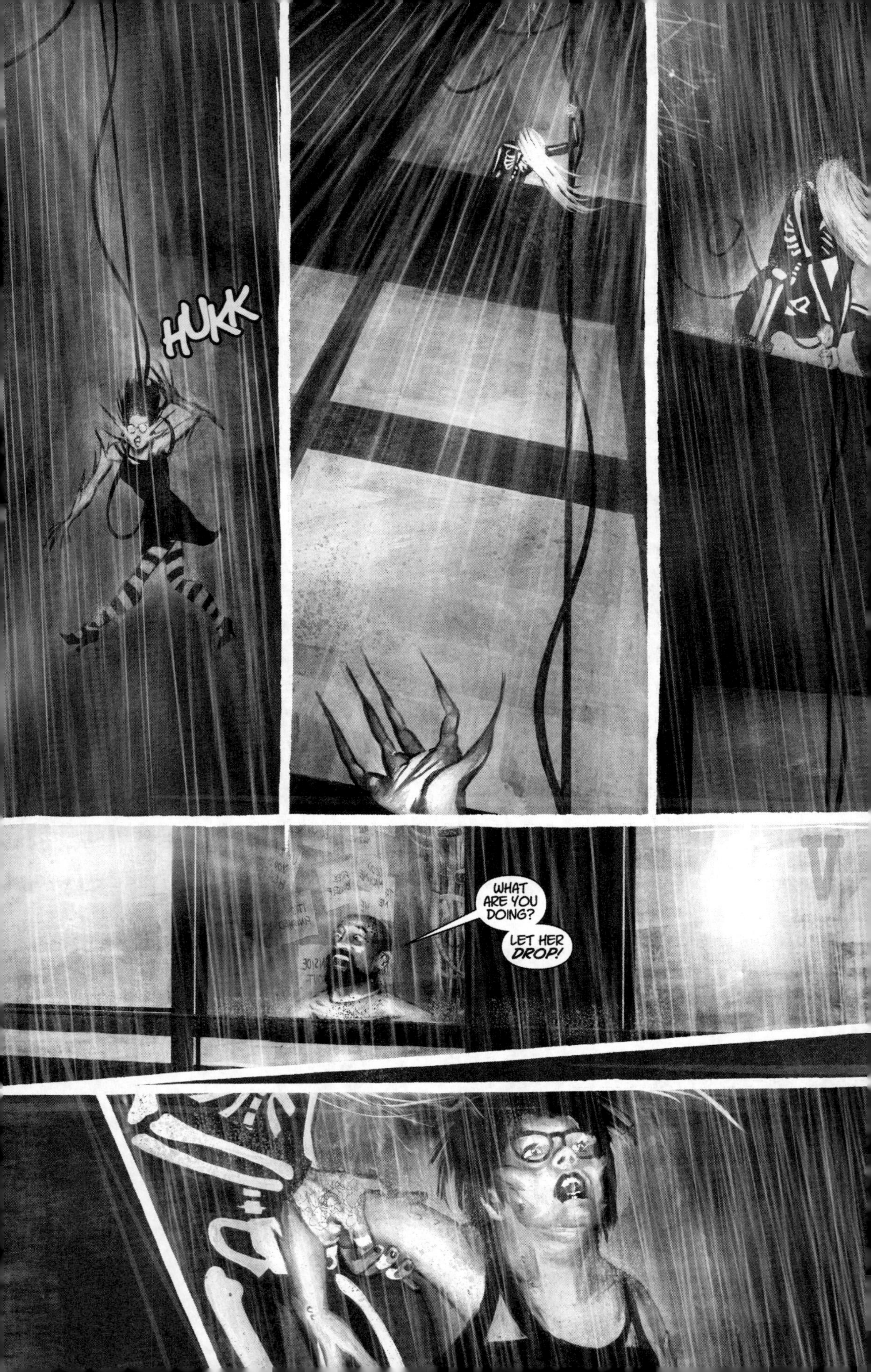
HUKK
WHAT ARE YOU DOING?
LET HER *DROP!*

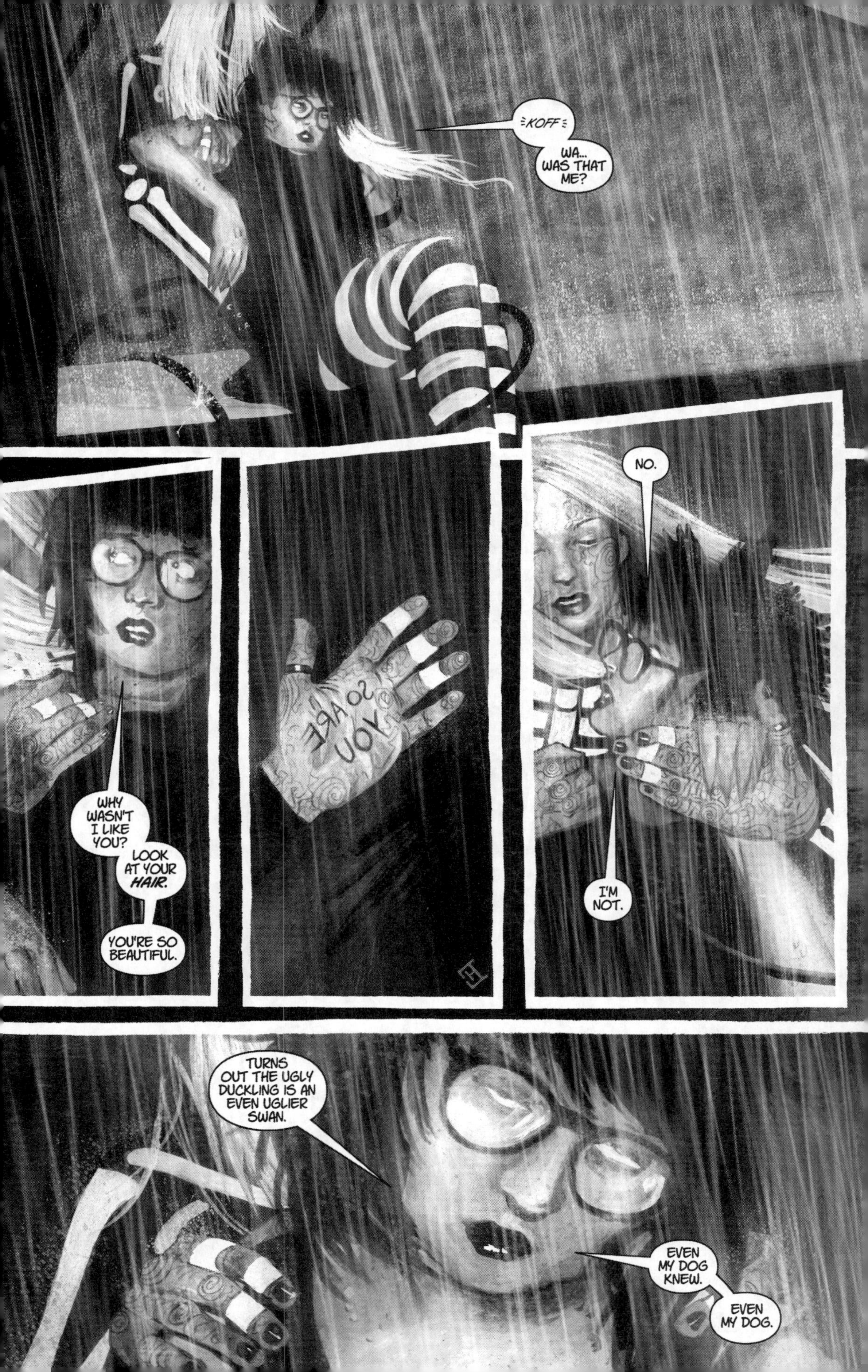

KOFF
WA... WAS THAT ME?
WHY WASN'T I LIKE YOU?
LOOK AT YOUR HAIR.
YOU'RE SO BEAUTIFUL.
SO ARE YOU
NO.
I'M NOT.
TURNS OUT THE UGLY DUCKLING IS AN EVEN UGLIER SWAN.
EVEN MY DOG KNEW.
EVEN MY DOG.

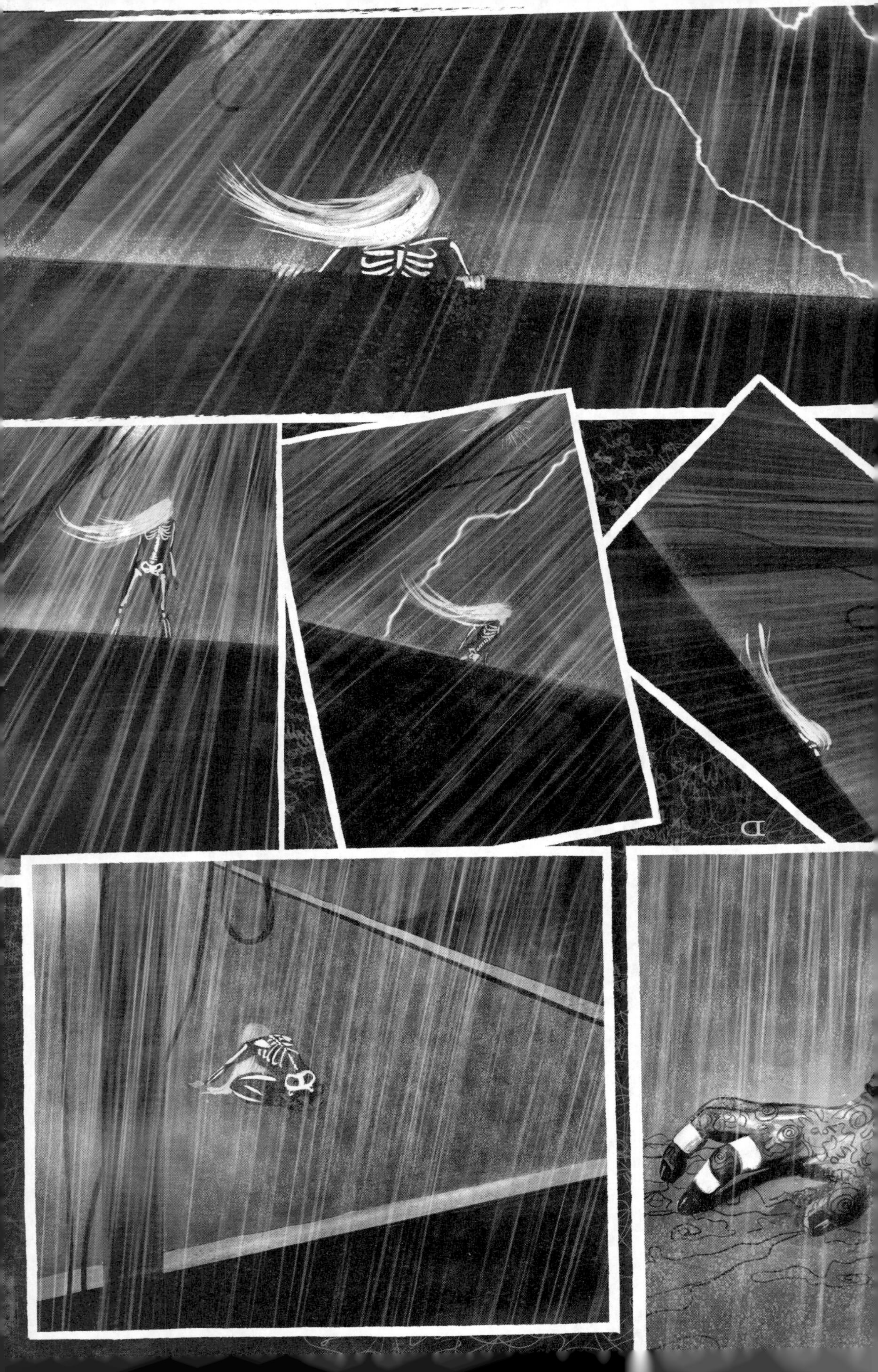

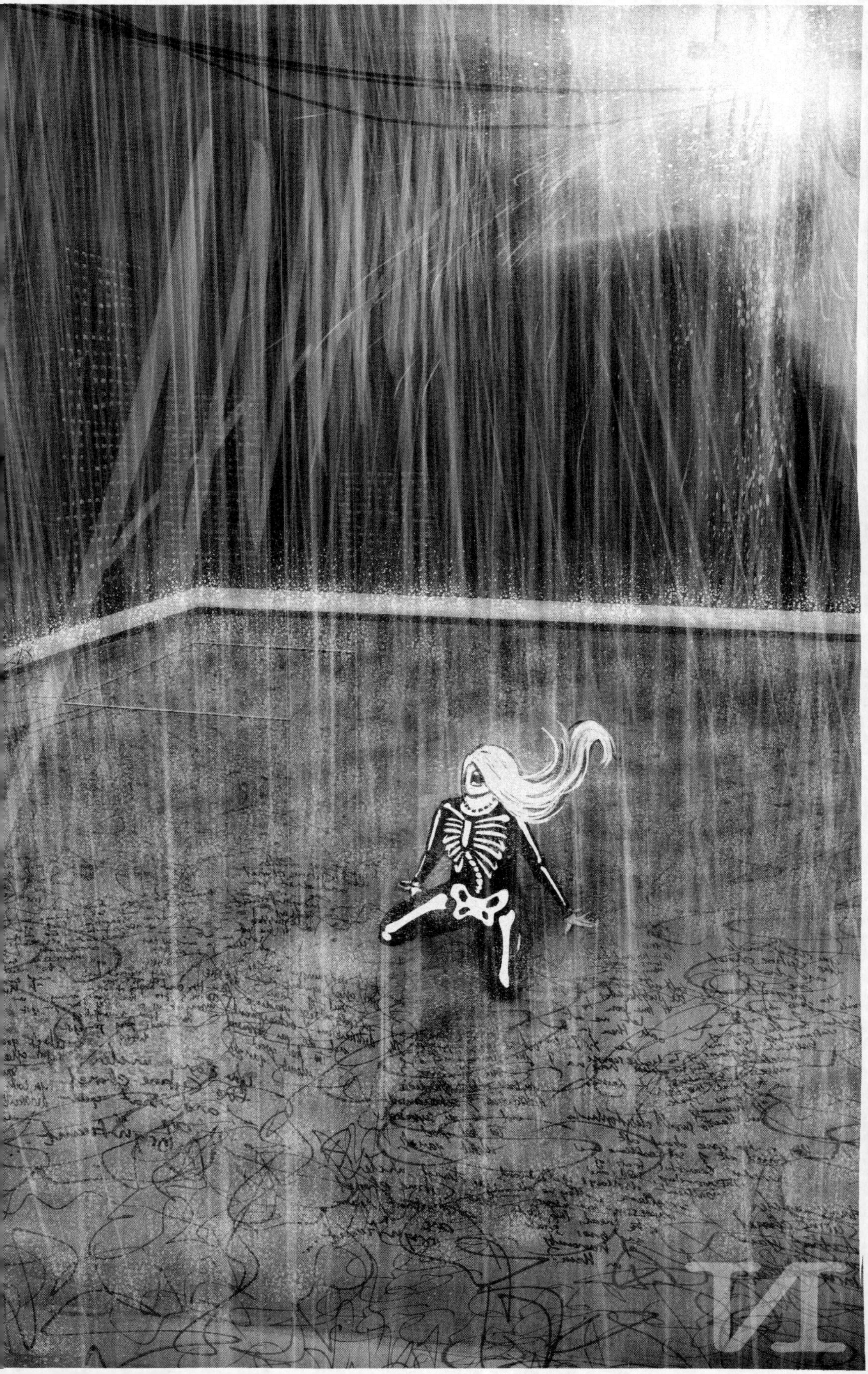

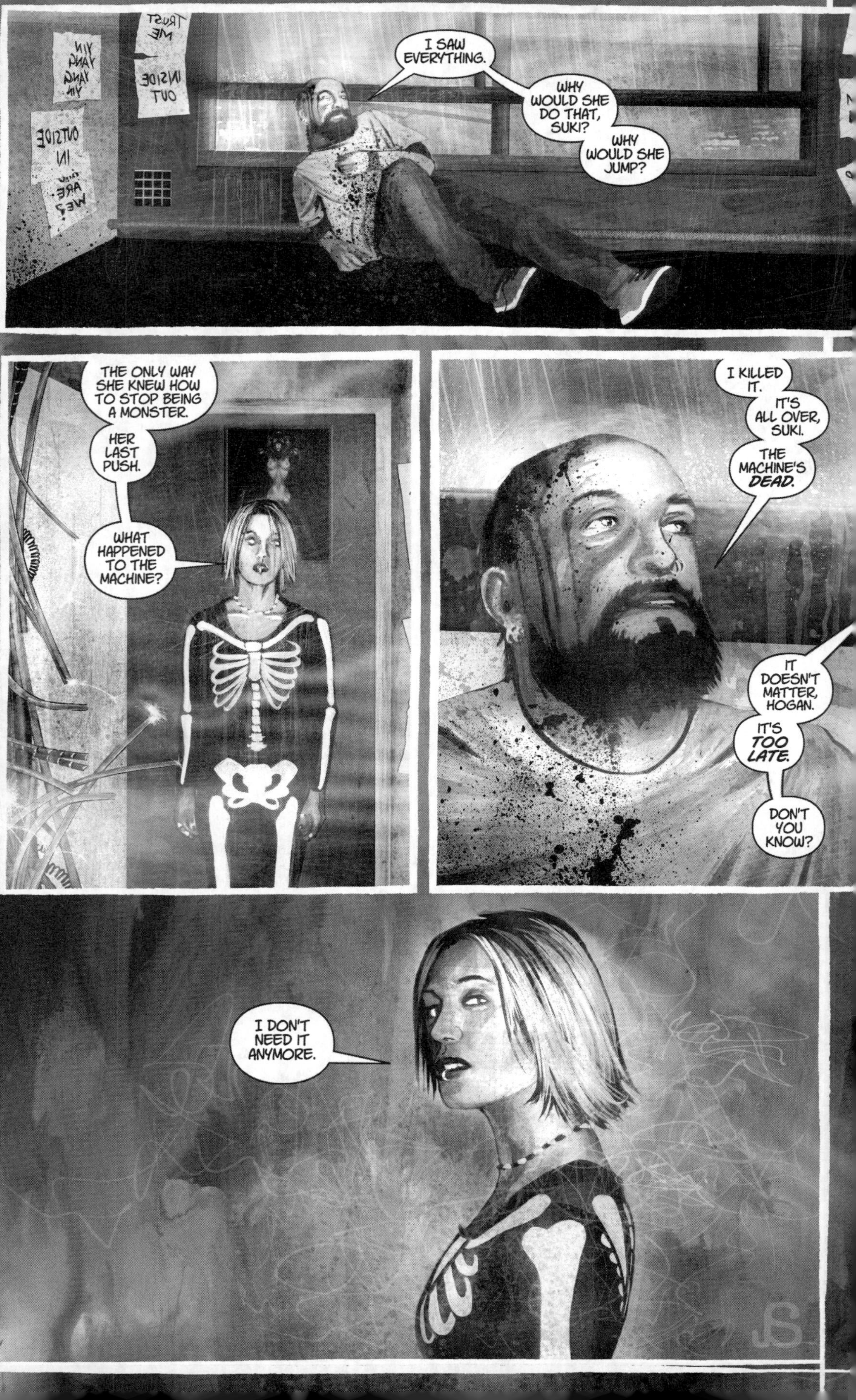
I SAW EVERYTHING.
WHY WOULD SHE DO THAT, SUKI?
WHY WOULD SHE JUMP?
THE ONLY WAY SHE KNEW HOW TO STOP BEING A MONSTER.
HER LAST PUSH.
WHAT HAPPENED TO THE MACHINE?
I KILLED IT.
IT'S ALL OVER, SUKI.
THE MACHINE'S DEAD.
IT DOESN'T MATTER, HOGAN.
IT'S TOO LATE.
DON'T YOU KNOW?
I DON'T NEED IT ANYMORE.

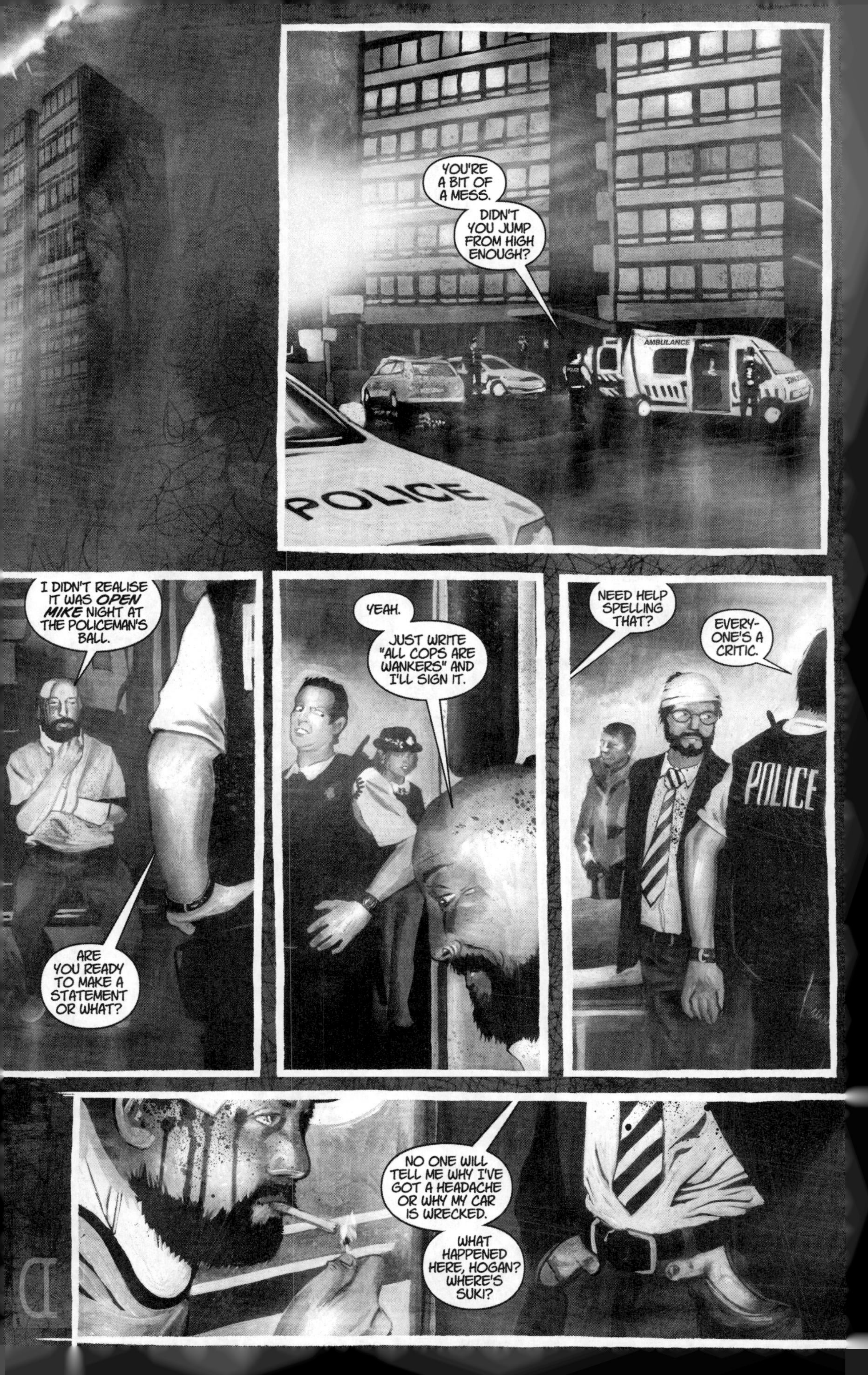
YOU'RE A BIT OF A MESS.
DIDN'T YOU JUMP FROM HIGH ENOUGH?
AMBULANCE
POLICE
I DIDN'T REALISE IT WAS *OPEN MIKE* NIGHT AT THE POLICEMAN'S BALL.
ARE YOU READY TO MAKE A STATEMENT OR WHAT?
YEAH.
JUST WRITE "ALL COPS ARE WANKERS" AND I'LL SIGN IT.
NEED HELP SPELLING THAT?
EVERY-ONE'S A CRITIC.
POLICE
NO ONE WILL TELL ME WHY I'VE GOT A HEADACHE OR WHY MY CAR IS WRECKED.
WHAT HAPPENED HERE, HOGAN? WHERE'S SUKI?

THIS HALFWAY HOUSE OF YOURS, DOC. IT'S NOT ALL IT'S CRACKED UP TO BE.

YOU TELL US LOONIES THAT WE'RE ALL WELCOME BACK TO OUR COSY LITTLE CELLS ANYTIME...

...BUT THE TRUTH IS, *NOBODY* GOES BACK.

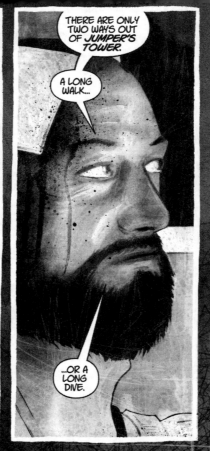

THERE ARE ONLY TWO WAYS OUT OF *JUMPER'S TOWER*.

A LONG WALK...

...OR A LONG DIVE.

SO WHICH WAY DO YOU PLAN ON GOING?

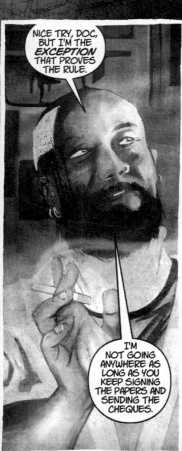

NICE TRY, DOC, BUT I'M THE *EXCEPTION* THAT PROVES THE RULE.

I'M NOT GOING ANYWHERE AS LONG AS YOU KEEP SIGNING THE PAPERS AND SENDING THE CHEQUES.

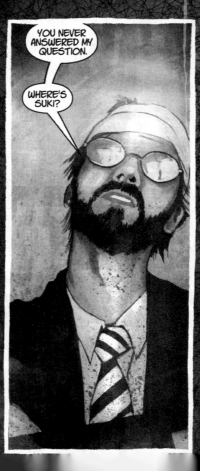

YOU NEVER ANSWERED MY QUESTION.

WHERE'S SUKI?

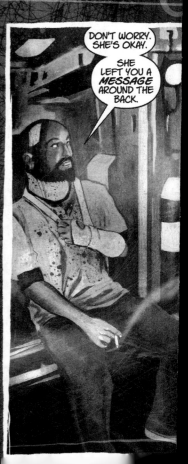

DON'T WORRY. SHE'S OKAY.

SHE LEFT YOU A *MESSAGE* AROUND THE BACK.

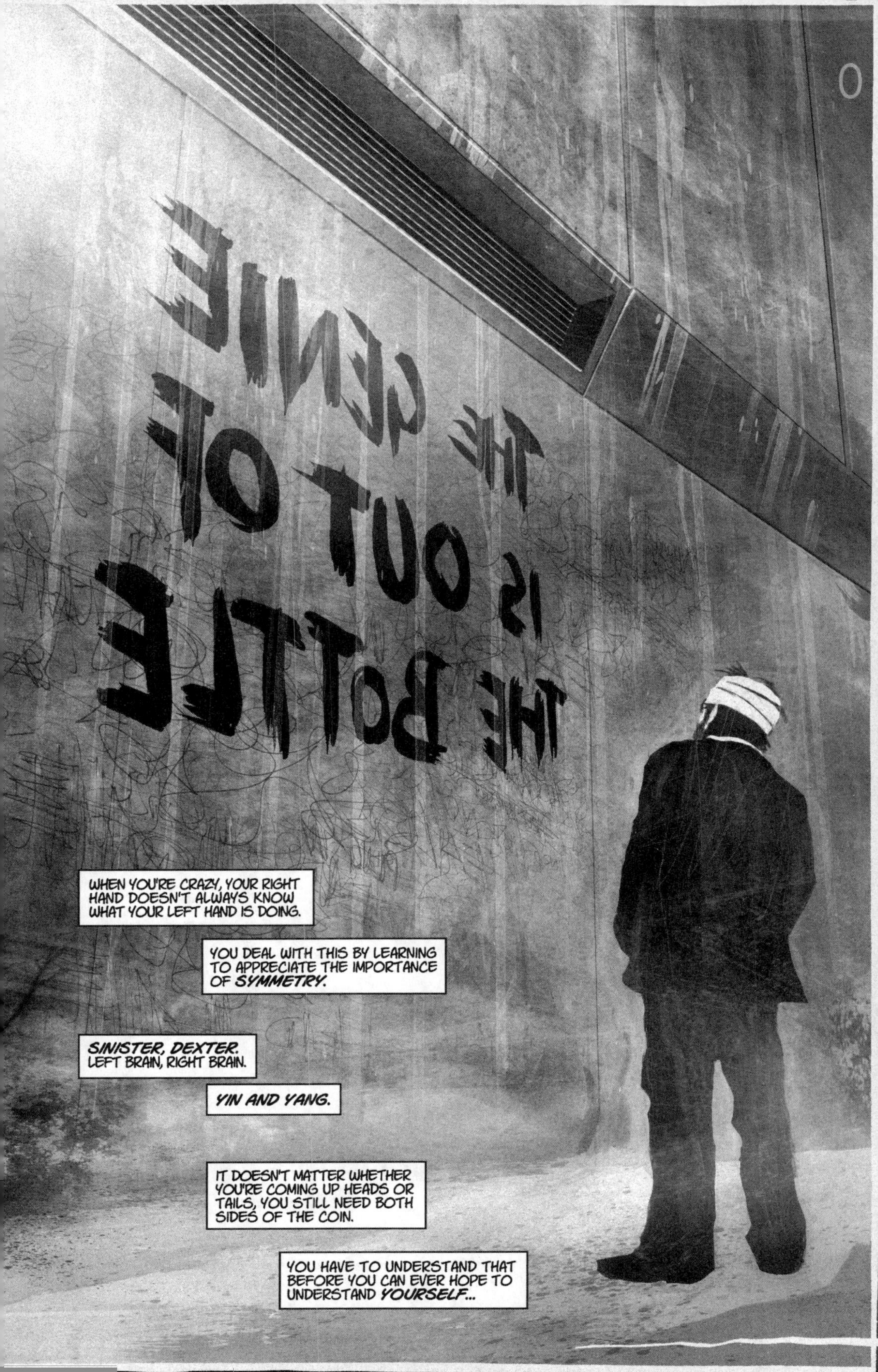
THE GENIE IS OUT OF THE BOTTLE
WHEN YOU'RE CRAZY, YOUR RIGHT HAND DOESN'T ALWAYS KNOW WHAT YOUR LEFT HAND IS DOING.
YOU DEAL WITH THIS BY LEARNING TO APPRECIATE THE IMPORTANCE OF *SYMMETRY*.
SINISTER, DEXTER. LEFT BRAIN, RIGHT BRAIN.
YIN AND YANG.
IT DOESN'T MATTER WHETHER YOU'RE COMING UP HEADS OR TAILS, YOU STILL NEED BOTH SIDES OF THE COIN.
YOU HAVE TO UNDERSTAND THAT BEFORE YOU CAN EVER HOPE TO UNDERSTAND *YOURSELF...*

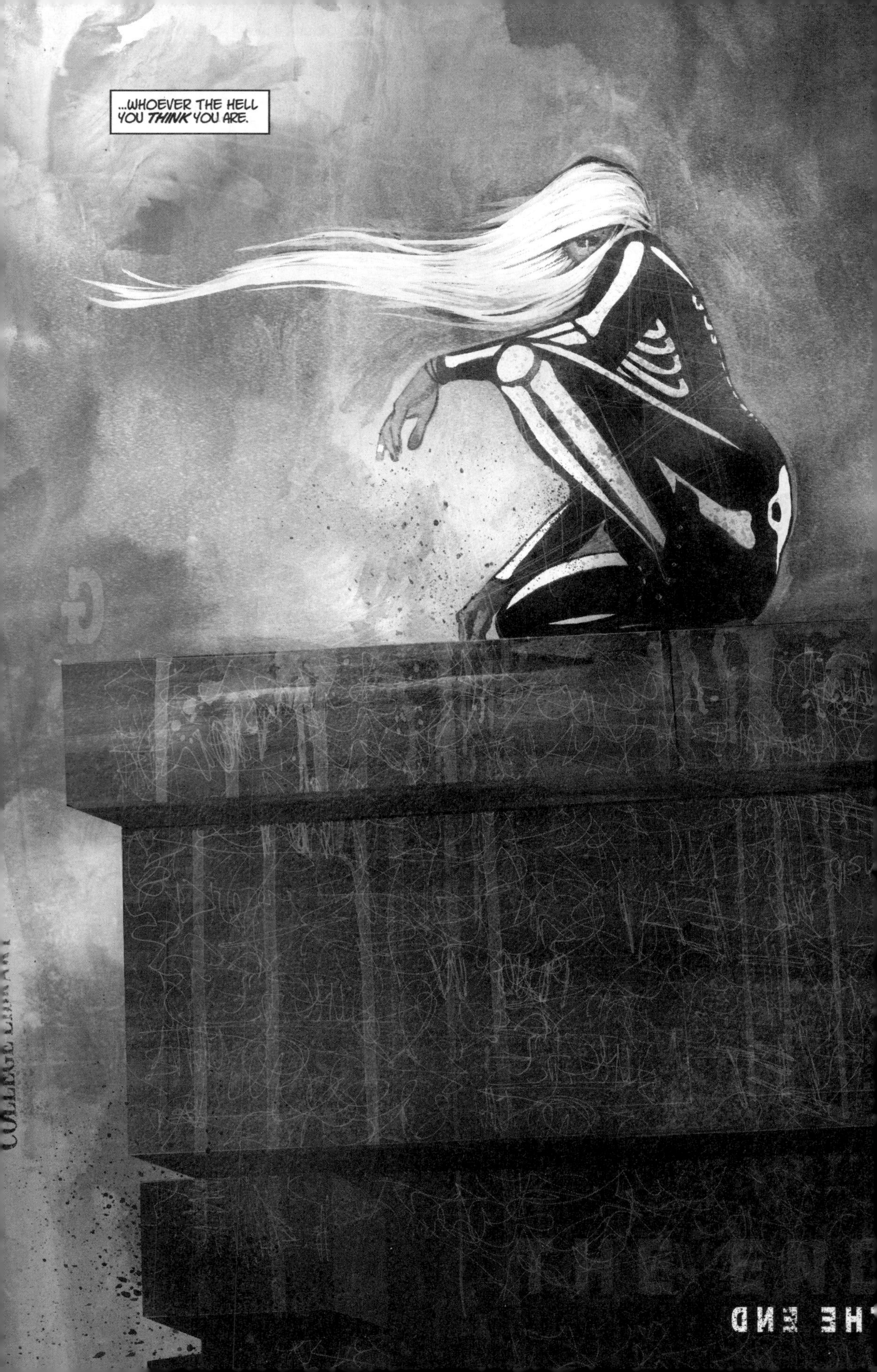
...WHOEVER THE HELL YOU *THINK* YOU ARE.